'And then he, completely astonished at her words, left off his lewdness, saying to her as many a man had done before, "Either you are a truly good woman or else a truly wicked woman."'

MARGERY KEMPE
Born *c.* 1373, Norfolk, England
Died *c.* 1438

Being illiterate, Margery Kempe had to rely on two men to
write down her autobiography – the first in English. Her
original scribe, an Englishman who had lived in Germany,
died before its completion; the second was a reluctant priest,
persuaded by Margery to finish the job in the late 1430s. This
volume includes selections from her book, which was lost for
centuries until its rediscovery in a family library in 1934.

KEMPE IN PENGUIN CLASSICS
The Book of Margery Kempe

MARGERY KEMPE

How To Be a Medieval Woman

Translated by
B. A. Windeatt

PENGUIN BOOKS

PENGUIN CLASSICS

UK | USA | Canada | Ireland | Australia
India | New Zealand | South Africa

Penguin Classics is part of the Penguin Random House group of companies
whose addresses can be found at global.penguinrandomhouse.com.

Penguin
Random House
UK

This selection first published in Penguin Classics in 2016
001

Translation copyright © B. A. Windeatt 1985, 1994, 2004

The moral right of the translator has been asserted

Set in 9.5/13 pt Baskerville 10 Pro
Typeset by Jouve (UK), Milton Keynes
Printed in Great Britain by Clays Ltd, St Ives plc

A CIP catalogue record for this book is available from the British Library

ISBN: 978-0-241-25226-0

www.greenpenguin.co.uk

Contents

Margery's Madness

When this creature was twenty years of age, or somewhat more, she was married to a worshipful burgess and was with child within a short time, as nature would have it. And after she had conceived, she was troubled with severe attacks of sickness until the child was born. And then, what with the labour-pains she had in childbirth and the sickness that had gone before, she despaired of her life, believing she might not live. Then she sent for her confessor, for she had a thing on her conscience which she had never revealed before that time in all her life. For she was continually hindered by her enemy – the devil – always saying to her while she was in good health that she didn't need to confess but to do penance by herself alone, and all should be forgiven, for God is merciful enough. And therefore this creature often did great penance in fasting on bread and water, and performed other acts of charity with devout prayers, but she would not reveal that one thing in confession.

And when she was at any time sick or troubled, the devil said in her mind that she should be damned, for she was not shriven of that fault. Therefore, after her child was born, and not believing she would live, she sent for her confessor, as said before, fully wishing to be shriven of her whole lifetime, as near as she could. And when she came to the point of saying that thing which she had so long concealed, her confessor was a little too hasty and began sharply to reprove her before she had fully said what she meant, and so she would say no more in spite of anything he might do. And soon after, because of the dread she had of damnation on the one hand, and his sharp reproving of her on the other, this creature went out of her mind and was amazingly disturbed and tormented with spirits for half a year, eight weeks and odd days.

And in this time she saw, as she thought, devils opening their mouths all alight with burning flames of fire, as if they would have swallowed her in, sometimes pawing at her, sometimes threatening her, sometimes pulling her and hauling her about both night and day during the said time. And also the devils called out to her with great threats, and bade her that she should forsake her Christian faith and belief, and deny her God, his mother, and all the saints in heaven, her good works and all good virtues, her father, her mother, and all her friends. And so she did. She slandered her husband, her friends, and her own self. She spoke many sharp and reproving words; she recognized no virtue nor goodness; she desired all wickedness; just as the spirits tempted her to say and do, so she said and did. She would have killed herself many a time as they stirred her to, and would have been damned with them in hell, and in witness of this she bit her own hand so violently that the mark could be seen for the rest of her life. And also she pitilessly tore the skin on her body near her heart with her nails, for she had no other implement, and she would have done something worse, except that she was tied up and forcibly restrained both day and night so that she could not do as she wanted.

And when she had long been troubled by these and many other temptations, so that people thought she should never have escaped from them alive, then one time as she lay by herself and her keepers were not with her, our merciful Lord Christ Jesus – ever to be trusted, worshipped be his name, never forsaking his servant in time of need – appeared to his creature who had forsaken him, in the likeness of a man, the most seemly, most beauteous, and most amiable that ever might be seen with man's eye, clad in a mantle of purple silk, sitting upon her bedside, looking upon her with so blessed a countenance that she was strengthened in all her spirits, and he said to her these words: 'Daughter, why have you forsaken me, and I never forsook you?'

And as soon as he had said these words, she saw truly how the air opened as bright as any lightning, and he ascended up into the air, not hastily and quickly, but beautifully and gradually, so that she could clearly behold him in the air until it closed up again.

And presently the creature grew as calm in her wits and her reason as she ever was before, and asked her husband, as soon as he came to her, if she could have the keys of the buttery to get her food and drink as she had done before. Her maids and her keepers advised him that he should not deliver up any keys to her, for they said she would only give away such goods as there were, because she did not know what she was saying, as they believed.

Nevertheless, her husband, who always had tenderness and compassion for her, ordered that they should give her the keys. And she took food and drink as her bodily strength would allow her, and she once again recognized her friends and her household, and everybody else who came to her in order to see how our Lord Jesus Christ had worked his grace in her – blessed may he be, who is ever near in tribulation. When people think he is far away from them he is very near through his grace. Afterwards this creature performed all her responsibilities wisely and soberly enough, except that she did not truly know our Lord's power to draw us to him.

Margery Goes into Business

And when this creature had thus through grace come again to her right mind, she thought she was bound to God and that she would be his servant. Nevertheless, she would not leave her pride or her showy manner of dressing, which she had previously been used to, either for her husband, or for any other person's advice. And yet she knew full well that people made many adverse comments about her, because she wore gold pipes on her head, and her hoods with the tippets were fashionably slashed. Her cloaks were also modishly slashed and underlaid with various colours between the slashes, so that she would be all the more stared at, and all the more esteemed.

And when her husband used to try and speak to her, to urge her to leave her proud ways, she answered sharply and shortly, and said that she was come of worthy kindred – he should never have married her – for her father was sometimes mayor of the town of N., and afterwards he was alderman of the High Guild of the Trinity in N. And therefore she would keep up the honour of her kindred, whatever anyone said.

She was enormously envious of her neighbours if they

were dressed as well as she was. Her whole desire was to be respected by people. She would not learn her lesson from a single chastening experience, nor be content with the worldly goods that God had sent her – as her husband was – but always craved more and more.

And then, out of pure covetousness, and in order to maintain her pride, she took up brewing, and was one of the greatest brewers in the town of N. for three or four years until she lost a great deal of money, for she had never had any experience in that business. For however good her servants were and however knowledgeable in brewing, things would never go successfully for them. For when the ale had as fine a head of froth on it as anyone might see, suddenly the froth would go flat, and all the ale was lost in one brewing after another, so that her servants were ashamed and would not stay with her. Then this creature thought how God had punished her before – and she could not take heed – and now again by the loss of her goods; and then she left off and did no more brewing.

And then she asked her husband's pardon because she would not follow his advice previously, and she said that her pride and sin were the cause of all her punishing, and that she would willingly put right all her wrongdoing. But yet she did not entirely give up the world, for she now thought up a new enterprise for herself. She had a horse-mill. She got herself two good horses and a man to grind people's corn, and thus she was confident of

making her living. This business venture did not last
long, for shortly afterwards, on the eve of Corpus Christi,
the following marvel happened. The man was in good
health, and his two horses were strong and in good con-
dition and had drawn well in the mill previously, but
now, when he took one of those horses and put him in
the mill as he had done before, this horse would not pull
in the mill in spite of anything the man might do. The
man was sorry, and tried everything he could think of to
make his horse pull. Sometimes he led him by the head,
sometimes he beat him, and sometimes he made a fuss
of him, but nothing did any good, for the horse would
rather go backwards than forwards. Then this man set a
pair of sharp spurs on his heels and rode on the horse's
back to make him pull, but it was no better. When this
man saw it was no use, he put the horse back in his stable,
and gave him food, and the horse ate well and freshly.
And afterwards he took the other horse and put him in
the mill. And just as his fellow had done so did he, for
he would not pull for anything the man might do. And
then this man gave up his job and would not stay any
longer with the said creature.

Then it was noised about in the town of N. that neither
man nor beast would serve the said creature, and some
said she was accursed; some said God openly took vengeance on her; some said one thing and some said
another. And some wise men, whose minds were more
grounded in the love of our Lord, said it was the high

mercy of our Lord Jesus Christ that called her from the pride and vanity of this wretched world.

And then this creature, seeing all these adversities coming on every side, thought they were the scourges of our Lord that would chastise her for her sin. Then she asked God for mercy, and forsook her pride, her covetousness, and the desire that she had for worldly dignity, and did great bodily penance, and began to enter the way of everlasting life as shall be told hereafter.

Full Merry in Heaven

One night, as this creature lay in bed with her husband, she heard a melodious sound so sweet and delectable that she thought she had been in paradise. And immediately she jumped out of bed and said, 'Alas that ever I sinned! It is full merry in heaven.' This melody was so sweet that it surpassed all the melody that might be heard in this world, without any comparison, and it caused this creature when she afterwards heard any mirth or melody to shed very plentiful and abundant tears of high devotion, with great sobbings and sighings for the bliss of heaven, not fearing the shames and contempt of this wretched world. And ever after her being drawn towards God in this way, she kept in mind the joy and the melody that there was in heaven, so much so that she could not very well restrain herself from speaking of it. For when she was in company with any people she would often say, 'It is full merry in heaven!'

And those who knew of her behaviour previously and now heard her talk so much of the bliss of heaven said to her, 'Why do you talk so of the joy that is in heaven? You don't know it, and you haven't been there any more than we have.' And they were angry with her because she would not hear or talk of worldly things as they did, and as she did previously.

And after this time she never had any desire to have sexual intercourse with her husband, for paying the debt of matrimony was so abominable to her that she would rather, she thought, have eaten and drunk the ooze and muck in the gutter than consent to intercourse, except out of obedience.

And so she said to her husband, 'I may not deny you my body, but all the love and affection of my heart is withdrawn from all earthly creatures and set on God alone.' But he would have his will with her, and she obeyed with much weeping and sorrowing because she could not live in chastity. And often this creature advised her husband to live chaste and said that they had often (she well knew) displeased God by their inordinate love, and the great delight that each of them had in using the other's body, and now it would be a good thing if by mutual consent they punished and chastised themselves by abstaining from the lust of their bodies. Her husband said it was good to do so, but he might not yet – he would do so when God willed. And so he used her as he had done before, he would not desist. And all the time she prayed to God that she might live chaste, and three or four years afterwards, when it pleased our Lord, her husband made a vow of chastity, as shall be written afterwards, by Jesus's leave.

And also, after this creature heard this heavenly melody, she did great bodily penance. She was sometimes shriven two or three times on the same day, especially of that sin which she had so long concealed and covered up, as is written at the beginning of this book. She gave herself up to much fasting and keeping of vigils; she rose at two or three of the clock and went to church, and was there at her prayers until midday and also the whole afternoon. And then she was slandered and reproved by many people because she led so strict a life. She got herself a hair-cloth from a kiln – the sort that malt is dried on – and put it inside her gown as discreetly and secretly as she could, so that her husband should not notice it. And nor did he, although she lay beside him every night in bed and wore the hair-shirt every day, and bore him children during that time.

Then she had three years of great difficulty with temptations, which she bore as meekly as she could, thanking our Lord for all his gifts, and she was as merry when she was reproved, scorned or ridiculed for our Lord's love, and much more merry than she was before amongst the dignities of this world. For she knew very well that she had sinned greatly against God and that she deserved far more shame and sorrow than any man could cause her, and contempt in this world was the right way heavenwards, for Christ himself chose that way. All his apostles, martyrs, confessors and virgins, and all those who ever came to heaven, passed by the way of tribulation, and she desired nothing as much as heaven. Then she was glad in her conscience when she believed that she was entering upon the way which would lead her to the place that she most desired.

And this creature had contrition and great compunction, with plentiful tears and much loud and violent sobbing, for her sins and for her unkindness towards her maker. She reflected on her unkindness since her childhood, as our Lord would put it into her mind, very many times. And then when she contemplated her own wickedness, she could only sorrow and weep and ever pray for mercy and forgiveness. Her weeping was so plentiful and so continual that many people thought that she could weep and leave off when she wanted, and therefore many people said she was a false hypocrite, and wept when in company for advantage and profit. And then very many people who loved her before while she was in the world abandoned her and would not know her, and all the while she thanked God for everything, desiring nothing but mercy and forgiveness of sin.

Margery Tempted

For the first two years when this creature was thus drawn to our Lord she had great quiet of spirit from any temptations. She could well endure fasting – it did not trouble her. She hated the joys of the world. She felt no rebellion in her flesh. She was so strong – as she thought – that she feared no devil in hell, for she performed such great bodily penance. She thought that she loved God more than he loved her. She was smitten with the deadly wound of vainglory and felt it not, for she desired many times that the crucifix should loosen his hands from the cross and embrace her in token of love. Our merciful Lord Christ Jesus, seeing this creature's presumption, sent her – as is written before – three years of great temptations, of one of the hardest of which I intend to write, as an example to those who come after that they should not trust in themselves nor have joy in themselves as this creature had – for undoubtedly our spiritual enemy does not sleep but busily probes our temperament and attitudes, and wherever he finds us most frail, there, by our Lord's sufferance, he lays his snare, which no one may escape by his own power.

And so he laid before this creature the snare of lechery, when she thought that all physical desire had been wholly quenched in her. And so she was tempted for a long time with the sin of lechery, in spite of anything she might do. Yet she was often shriven, she wore her hair-shirt, and did great bodily penance and wept many a bitter tear, and often prayed to our Lord that he should preserve her and keep her so that she should not fall into temptation, for she thought she would rather have been dead than consent to that. And in all this time she had no desire to have intercourse with her husband, and it was very painful and horrible to her.

In the second year of her temptations it so happened that a man whom she liked said to her on St Margaret's Eve before evensong that, for anything, he would sleep with her and enjoy the lust of his body, and that she should not withstand him, for if he might not have his desire that time, he said, he would have it another time instead – she should not choose. And he did it to test what she would do, but she imagined that he meant it in earnest and said very little in reply. So they parted then and both went to hear evensong, for her church was dedicated to St Margaret. This woman was so troubled with the man's words that she could not listen to evensong, nor say her paternoster, nor think any other good thought, but was more troubled than she ever was before.

The devil put it into her mind that God had forsaken her, or else she would not be so tempted. She believed the devil's persuasions, and began to consent because she could not think any good thought. Therefore she believed that God had forsaken her. And when evensong was over, she went to the said man, in order that he should have his will of her, as she believed he desired, but he put forward such a pretence that she could not understand his intent, and so they parted for that night. This creature was so troubled and vexed all that night that she did not know what she could do. She lay beside her husband, and to have intercourse with him was so abominable to her that she could not bear it, and yet it was permissible for her and at a rightful time if she had wished it. But all the time she was tormented to sin with the other man because he had spoken to her. At last – through the importunings of temptation and a lack of discretion – she was overcome and consented in her mind, and went to the man to know if he would then consent to have her. And he said he would not for all the wealth in this world; he would rather be chopped up as small as meat for the pot.

She went away all ashamed and confused in herself, seeing his steadfastness and her own instability. Then she thought about the grace that God had given her before, of how she had two years of great quiet in her soul, of repentance for her sins with many bitter tears of compunction, and a perfect will never again to turn to sin but rather, she thought, to be dead. And now she saw how she had consented in her will to sin. Then she half fell into despair. She thought herself in hell, such was the sorrow that she had. She thought she was worthy of no mercy because her consenting to sin was so wilfully done, nor ever worthy to serve God, because she was so false to him.

Nevertheless she was shriven many times and often, and did whatever penance her confessor would enjoin her to do, and was governed according to the rules of the Church. That grace God gave this creature – blessed may he be – but he did not withdraw her temptation, but rather increased it, as she thought.

And therefore she thought that he had forsaken her, and dared not trust to his mercy, but was troubled with horrible temptations to lechery and despair nearly all the following year, except that our Lord in his mercy, as she said to herself, gave her every day for the most part two hours of compunction for her sins, with many bitter tears. And afterwards she was troubled with temptations to despair as she was before, and was as far from feelings of grace as those who never felt any. And that she could not bear, and so she continued to despair. Except for the time that she felt grace, her trials were so amazing that she could not cope very well with them, but always mourned and sorrowed as though God had forsaken her.

A Pledge of Paradise

Then on a Friday before Christmas Day, as this creature was kneeling in a chapel of St John, within a church of St Margaret in N., weeping a very great deal and asking mercy and forgiveness for her sins and her trespasses, our merciful Lord Christ Jesus – blessed may he be – ravished her spirit and said to her, 'Daughter, why are you weeping so sorely? I have come to you, Jesus Christ, who died on the cross suffering bitter pains and passion for you. I, the same God, forgive you your sins to the uttermost point. And you shall never come into hell nor into purgatory, but when you pass out of this world, within the twinkling of an eye, you shall have the bliss of heaven, for I am the same God who has brought your sins to your mind and caused you to be shriven of them. And I grant you contrition until your life's end.

'Therefore, I command you, boldly call me Jesus, your love, for I am your love and shall be your love without end. And, daughter, you have a hair-shirt on your back. I want you to leave off wearing it, and I shall give you a hair-shirt in your heart which shall please me much more than all the hair-shirts in the world. But also, my beloved daughter, you must give up that which you love best in this world, and that is the eating of meat. And instead of meat you shall eat my flesh and my blood, that is the true body of Christ in the sacrament of the altar. This is my will, daughter, that you receive my body every Sunday, and I shall cause so much grace to flow into you that everyone shall marvel at it.

'You shall be eaten and gnawed by the people of the world just as any rat gnaws the stockfish. Don't be afraid, daughter, for you shall be victorious over all your enemies. I shall give you grace enough to answer every cleric in the love of God. I swear to you by my majesty that I shall never forsake you whether in happiness or in sorrow. I shall help you and protect you, so that no devil in hell shall ever part you from me, nor angel in heaven, nor man on earth – for devils in hell may not, nor angels in heaven will not, nor man on earth shall not.

'And daughter, I want you to give up your praying of many beads, and think such thoughts as I shall put into your mind. I shall give you leave to pray until six o'clock to say what you wish. Then you shall lie still and speak to me in thought, and I shall give you high meditation and true contemplation. And I command you to go to the anchorite at the Preaching Friars and tell him my confidences and counsels which I reveal to you, and do as he advises, for my spirit shall speak in him to you.'

Then this creature went off to see the anchorite as she was commanded, and revealed to him the revelations that

had been shown to her. Then the anchorite, with great
reverence and weeping, thanking God, said, 'Daughter,
you are sucking even at Christ's breast, and you have
received a pledge of paradise. I charge you to receive
such thoughts – when God will give them – as meekly
and devoutly as you can, and then come and tell me what
they are, and I shall, by the leave of our Lord Jesus
Christ, tell you whether they are from the Holy Ghost or
else from your enemy the devil.'

Spiritual Health

Soon after, this creature was moved in her soul to go and visit certain places for spiritual health, in as much as she was cured; and she could not without the consent of her husband. She asked her husband to grant her leave and he, fully believing it was the will of God, soon consented, and they went together to such places as she was inclined.

And then our Lord Christ Jesus said to her, 'My servants greatly desire to see you.'

Then she was welcomed and made much of in various places, and because of this she had a great fear of vainglory and was much afraid. Our merciful Lord Christ Jesus – worshipped be his name – said to her, 'Don't be afraid, daughter – I shall take vainglory from you. For they that honour you honour me; they that despise you despise me, and I shall chastise them for it. I am in you, and you in me. And they that hear you, they hear the voice of God. Daughter, there is no man so sinful alive on earth that, if he will give up his sin and do as you advise, then such grace as you promise him I will confirm for love of you.' Then her husband and she went on to York and to other different places.

No Good Wife

It happened one Friday, Midsummer Eve, in very hot weather – as this creature was coming from York carrying a bottle of beer in her hand, and her husband a cake tucked inside his clothes against his chest – that her husband asked his wife this question: 'Margery, if there came a man with a sword who would strike off my head unless I made love with you as I used to do before, tell me on your conscience – for you say you will not lie – whether you would allow my head to be cut off, or else allow me to make love with you again, as I did at one time?'

'Alas, sir,' she said, 'why are you raising this matter, when we have been chaste for these past eight weeks?'

'Because I want to know the truth of your heart.'

And then she said with great sorrow, 'Truly, I would rather see you being killed, than that we should turn back to our uncleanness.'

And he replied, 'You are no good wife.'

And then she asked her husband what was the reason that he had not made love to her for the last eight weeks, since she lay with him every night in his bed. And he said that he was made so afraid when he would have touched her, that he dared do no more.

'Now, good sir, mend your ways and ask God's mercy, for I told you nearly three years ago that you[r desire for sex] would suddenly be slain – and this is now the third year, and I hope yet that I shall have my wish. Good sir, I pray you to grant what I shall ask, and I shall pray for you to be saved through the mercy of our Lord Jesus Christ, and you shall have more reward in heaven than if you wore a hair-shirt or wore a coat of mail as a penance. I pray you, allow me to make a vow of chastity at whichever bishop's hand that God wills.'

'No,' he said, 'I won't allow you to do that, because now I can make love to you without mortal sin, and then I wouldn't be able to.'

Then she replied, 'If it be the will of the Holy Ghost to fulfil what I have said, I pray God that you may consent to this; and if it be not the will of the Holy Ghost, I pray God that you never consent.'

Then they went on towards Bridlington and the weather was extremely hot, this creature all the time having great sorrow and great fear for her chastity. And as they came by a cross her husband sat down under the cross, calling his wife to him and saying these words to her: 'Margery, grant me my desire, and I shall grant you your desire. My first desire is that we shall still lie together in one bed as we have done before; the second, that you shall pay my debts before you go to Jerusalem; and the third, that you shall eat and drink with me on Fridays as you used to do.'

'No, sir,' she said, 'I will never agree to break my Friday fast as long as I live.'

'Well,' he said, 'then I'm going to have sex with you again.'

She begged him to allow her to say her prayers, and he kindly allowed it. Then she knelt down beside a cross in the field and prayed in this way, with a great abundance of tears: 'Lord God, you know all things. You know what sorrow I have had to be chaste for you in my body all these three years, and now I might have my will and I dare not, for love of you. For if I were to break that custom of fasting from meat and drink on Fridays which you commanded me, I should now have my desire. But, blessed Lord, you know I will not go against your will, and great is my sorrow now unless I find comfort in you. Now, blessed Jesus, make your will known to my unworthy self, so that I may afterwards follow and fulfil it with all my might.'

And then our Lord Jesus Christ with great sweetness spoke to this creature, commanding her to go again to her husband and pray him to grant her what she desired: 'And he shall have what he desires. For, my beloved daughter, this was the reason why I ordered you to fast, so that you should the sooner obtain your desire, and now it is granted to you. I no longer wish you to fast, and therefore I command you in the name of Jesus to eat and drink as your husband does.'

Then this creature thanked our Lord Jesus Christ for his grace and his goodness, and afterwards got up and went to her husband, saying to him, 'Sir, if you please, you shall grant me my desire, and you shall have your desire. Grant me that you will not come into my bed, and I grant you that I will pay your debts before I go to Jerusalem. And make my body free to God, so that you never make any claim on me requesting any conjugal debt after this day as long as you live – and I shall eat and drink on Fridays at your bidding.'

Then her husband replied to her, 'May your body be as freely available to God as it has been to me.'

This creature thanked God greatly, rejoicing that she had her desire, praying her husband that they should say three paternosters in worship of the Trinity for the great grace that had been granted them. And so they did, kneeling under a cross, and afterwards they ate and drank together in great gladness of spirit. This was on a Friday, on Midsummer's Eve.

Then they went on to Bridlington and also to many other places, and spoke with God's servants, both anchorites and recluses, and many other of our Lord's lovers, with many worthy clerics, doctors and bachelors of divinity as well, in many different places. And to various people amongst them this creature revealed her feelings and her contemplations, as she was commanded to do, to find out if there were any deception in her feelings.

Enclosed in a House of Stone

On one occasion, when this creature was at Canterbury in the church amongst the monks, she was greatly despised and reproved because she wept so much – both by the monks and priests, and by secular men, nearly all day, both morning and afternoon – and so much so that her husband went away from her as if he had not known her, and left her alone among them, choose how she might, for no further comfort did she have from him that day.

So an old monk, who had been treasurer to the Queen when he was in secular clothes, a powerful man and greatly feared by many people, took her by the hand saying to her, 'What can you say of God?'

'Sir,' she said, 'I will both speak of him and hear of him,' repeating to the monk a story from scripture.

The monk said, 'I wish you were enclosed in a house of stone, so that no one should speak with you.'

'Ah, sir,' she said, 'you should support God's servants, and you are the first that hold against them – our Lord amend you.'

Then a young monk said to this creature, 'Either you have the Holy Ghost or else you have a devil within you, for what you are speaking here to us is Holy Writ, and that you do not have of yourself.'

Then this creature said, 'I pray you, sir, give me leave to tell you a tale.'

Then people said to the monk, 'Let her say what she wants.'

And then she said, 'There was once a man who had sinned greatly against God and, when he was shriven, his confessor enjoined him as part of his penance that he should for one year hire men to chide him and reprove him for his sins, and he should give them silver for their labour. And one day he came amongst many great men, such as are here now – God save you all – and stood among them as I now stand amongst you, they despising him as you do me, the man all the while laughing and smiling and having good sport at their words. The chief among them said to the man, "Why are you laughing, you wretch, when you are being greatly despised?"

'"Ah, sir, I have great cause to laugh, because I have for many days been taking silver from my purse and hiring men to chide me for remission of my sin, and today I can keep my silver in my purse, I thank you all."

'Right so I say to you, worshipful sirs. While I was at home in my own part of the country – day by day with great weeping and mourning – I sorrowed because I did not have any of the shame, scorn and contempt that I deserved. I thank you all highly, sirs, for what, morning and afternoon, I have received today in rightful measure – blessed be God for it.'

Then she went out of the monastery, they following and crying upon her, 'You shall be burnt, you false Lollard! Here is a cartful of thorns ready for you, and a barrel to burn you with!'

And the creature stood outside the gates of Canterbury – for it was in the evening – with many people wondering at her.

Then people said, 'Take her and burn her!'

And the creature stood still, her body trembling and quaking dreadfully – without any comfort in this world – and she did not know where her husband had gone.

Then she prayed in her heart to our Lord, thinking to herself in this way: 'I came to this place, Lord, for love of you. Blessed Lord, help me and have mercy on me.'

And then, after she had made her prayers in her heart to our Lord, there came two handsome young men and said to her, 'Are you neither a heretic nor a Lollard?'

And she said, 'No, sirs, I am neither heretic nor Lollard.'

Then they asked her where her inn was. She said she didn't know in which street, but anyway it would be at a German man's house. Then these two young men escorted her home to her lodgings and were very nice to her, asking her to pray for them – and there she found her husband.

And many people in N. had maligned her while she

was away, and slandered her in respect of many things that she was supposed to have done.

Then after this she was very much at rest in her soul for a long while, and had high contemplation day by day, and many a holy speech and confabulation with our Lord Jesus Christ both morning and afternoon, with many sweet tears of high devotion so abundantly and continually that it was a marvel that her eyes endured, or that her heart could last without being consumed with the ardour of love which was kindled with the holy converse of our Lord, when he said to her many times, 'Beloved daughter, love me with all your heart, for I love you with all my heart and with all the might of my Godhead, for you were a chosen soul without beginning in my sight and a pillar of Holy Church. My merciful eyes are ever upon you. It would be impossible for you to suffer the scorn and contempt that you will have, were it not for my grace supporting you.'

Margery Decides to Travel

This creature, when our Lord had forgiven her her sin (as has been written before), had a desire to see those places where he was born, and where he suffered his Passion and where he died, together with other holy places where he was during his life, and also after his resurrection.

While she was feeling these desires, our Lord commanded her in her mind – two years before she went – that she should go to Rome, to Jerusalem, and to Santiago de Compostela, and she would gladly have gone, but she had no money to go with.

And then she said to our Lord, 'Where shall I get the money to go to these holy places with?'

Our Lord replied to her, 'I shall send you enough friends in different parts of England to help you. And, daughter, I shall go with you in every country and provide for you. I shall lead you there and bring you back again in safety, and no Englishman shall die in the ship that you are in. I shall keep you from all wicked men's power. And, daughter, I say to you that I want you to wear white clothes and no other colour, for you shall dress according to my will.'

'Ah, dear Lord, if I go around dressed differently from how other chaste women dress, I fear people will slander me. They will say I am a hypocrite and ridicule me.'

'Yes, daughter, the more ridicule that you have for love of me, the more you please me.'

Then this creature dared not do otherwise than as she was commanded in her soul. And so she set off on her travels with her husband, for he was always a good and easygoing man with her. Although he sometimes – out of groundless fear – left her on her own for a while, yet he always came back to her again, and felt sorry for her, and spoke up for her as much as he dared for fear of other people. But all others that went along with her forsook her, and they most falsely accused her – through temptation of the devil – of things that she was never guilty of.

And so did one man in whom she greatly trusted, and who offered to travel with her, at which she was very pleased, believing he would give her support and help her when she needed it, for he had been staying a long time with an anchorite, a doctor of divinity and a holy man, and that anchorite was this woman's confessor.

And so his servant – at his own inward stirring – took his leave to travel with this creature; and her own maid-servant went with her too, for as long as things went well with them and nobody said anything against them.

But as soon as people – through the enticing of our spiritual enemy, and by permission of our Lord – spoke against this creature because she wept so grievously, and said she was a false hypocrite and deceived people, and threatened her with burning, then this man, who was held to be so holy, and in whom she trusted so much, rebuked her with the utmost force and scorned her most foully, and would not go any further with her. Her maidservant, seeing discomfort on every side, grew obstreperous with her mistress. She would not do as she was told, or follow her mistress's advice. She let her mistress go alone into many fine towns and would not go with her.

And always, her husband was ready when everybody else let her down, and he went with her where our Lord would send her, always believing that all was for the best, and would end well when God willed.

I Love You as Much as Any Maiden

At the time that this creature had revelations, our Lord said to her, 'Daughter, you are with child.'

She replied, 'Ah, Lord, what shall I do about looking after my child?'

Our Lord said, 'Daughter, don't be afraid, I shall arrange for it to be looked after.'

'Lord, I am not worthy to hear you speak, and still to make love with my husband, even though it is great pain and great distress to me.'

'Therefore it is no sin for you, daughter, because it is reward and merit instead for you, and you will not have any the less grace, for I wish you to bring me forth more fruit.'

Then the creature said, 'Lord Jesus, this manner of life belongs to your holy maidens.'

'Yes, daughter, but rest assured that I love wives also, and specially those wives who would live chaste if they might have their will, and do all they can to please me as you do. For though the state of maidenhood be more perfect and more holy than the state of widowhood, and the state of widowhood more perfect than the state of wedlock, yet I love you, daughter, as much as any maiden in the world. No man may prevent me from loving whom I wish and as much as I wish, for love, daughter, quenches all sin. And therefore ask of me the gifts of love. There is no gift so holy as is the gift of love, nor anything so much to be desired as love, for love may gain what it desires. And therefore, daughter, you may please God no better than to think continually on his love.'

Then this creature asked our Lord Jesus how she should best love him, and our Lord said, 'Be mindful of your wickedness, and think of my goodness.'

She replied, 'I am the most unworthy creature that you ever showed grace to on earth.'

'Ah, daughter,' said our Lord, 'do not be afraid. I take no notice of what a man has been, but I take heed of what he will be. Daughter, you have despised yourself; therefore you will never be despised by God. Bear in mind, daughter, what Mary Magdalene was, Mary of Egypt, St Paul, and many other saints that are now in heaven, for of unworthy, I make worthy, and of sinful, I make righteous. And so I have made you worthy to me, once loved and evermore loved by me. There is no saint in heaven that you wish to speak with, but he shall come to you. Whom God loves, they love. When you please God, you please his mother and all the saints in heaven. Daughter, I take witness of my mother, of all the angels in heaven, and of all the saints in heaven, that I love you with all my heart, and I may not forgo your love.'

Our Lord said then to his blessed mother, 'Blessed Mother, tell my daughter of the greatness of love I have for her.'

Then this creature lay still, weeping and sobbing as if her heart would burst for the sweetness of speech that our Lord spoke to her soul.

Immediately afterwards, the Queen of Mercy, God's mother, chatted to the soul of the creature, saying, 'My beloved daughter, I bring you sure tidings, bearing witness for my sweet son Jesus, with all angels and all saints in heaven who love you most highly. Daughter, I am your mother, your lady and your mistress, to teach you in every way how you shall please God best.'

She taught this creature and informed her so marvellously that she was embarrassed to tell it to anybody, the matter was so high and so holy, except to the anchorite who was her principal confessor, for he was most knowledgeable in such things. And he charged this creature – by virtue of obedience – to tell him whatever she felt, and so she did.

Charity Starts at Home

The priest who wrote down this book, in order to test this creature's feelings, asked her questions many different times about things that were to come – things of which the outcome was unsure and uncertain to anybody at that time – asking her, though she was loath and unwilling to do such things, to pray to God and discover when our Lord would visit her with devotion, what the outcome would be, and then truly, without any pretending, tell him how she felt, or else he would not have gladly written the book.

And so this creature, partly compelled by the fear that he would not otherwise have followed her intention in writing this book, did as he asked her and told him her feelings as to what would happen in such matters as he asked her about, if her feelings were true. And in this way he tested them for their truth. And yet he would not always give credence to her words, and that hindered him in the following way.

It happened once that a young man came to this priest, whom the priest had never seen before, bemoaning the poverty and trouble that had befallen him through bad

luck, explaining the cause of his misfortune, and also
saying he had taken holy orders to be a priest. Because
of a little over-hastiness in defending himself – as he had
no choice unless he was to be chased and killed by his
enemies – he struck a man, or else two, as a result of
which, as he said, they were dead or else likely to die.
And so he had fallen into an irregular life and might not
execute his orders without dispensation of the court of
Rome, and for this reason he fled from his friends, and
dared not go back to his part of the country for fear of
being arrested for their deaths.

The said priest gave credence to the young man's story
because he was a likeable person, handsome, well-favoured
in looks and manner, sober in talk, priestly in bearing
and dress. And feeling sorry for his trouble, and intending to get him some friends to relieve and comfort him,
he went to a respectable burgess in Lynn, the equal of
any mayor and a compassionate man, who was very ill
and had been for a long time. The priest lamented to this
man and to his wife, a very good woman, the bad luck
of this young man, believing he would receive a generous
donation, as he often had previously when he asked on
behalf of others.

It so happened that the creature of whom this book is
written was present there and heard how the priest put
the young man's case and praised him. And she was very
much moved in her spirit against that young man, and
said they had many poor neighbours whom they knew

well enough had great need to be helped and relieved, and it should rather be charity to help those whom they well knew to be well-disposed folk and their own neighbours than other strangers whom they did not know, for many speak and seem very fair outwardly to people's sight – God knows what they are in their souls!

The good man and his wife thought that she spoke very well, and therefore they would give him no charity. At that time the priest was very displeased with this creature, and when he met her alone he repeated how she had hindered him so that he could get no help for the young man, who was a well-disposed man, he thought, and he much commended his behaviour.

The creature said, 'Sir, God knows what his conduct is, for – as far as I know – I never saw him. And yet I have an understanding of what his conduct might be, and therefore, sir, if you will act according to my advice and to what I feel, let him choose and help himself as well as he can, and don't you get involved with him, for he will deceive you in the end.'

The young man was always going to see the priest, flattering him and saying that he had good friends in other places who would help him if they knew where he was – and that in a short time – and also they would thank those people who had supported him in his trouble. The priest, trusting that it would be as this young man told him, willingly lent him silver to help him out. The young man asked the priest to excuse him if he did not

see him for two or three days, because he was going a
little way away and would return shortly and bring him
back his silver, truly. The priest, having confidence in his
promise, was quite content, granting him love and leave
until the day when he had promised to come back again.

When he was gone, the said creature, having understanding by feeling in her soul that our Lord would show
that he was a dishonest man and would not come back
any more, she, to prove whether her feeling was true
or false, asked the priest where the young man was, that
he had praised so much. The priest said he had gone a
little way away, and he trusted that he would come back.
She said she supposed that he would not see him any
more, and nor did he ever again. And then he regretted
that he had not done as she advised.

Margery Sets Out

When the time came that this creature should visit those holy places where our Lord lived and died, as she had seen by revelation years before, she asked the parish priest of the town where she was living to say on her behalf from the pulpit that, if there were any man or woman who claimed any debt against her husband or her, they should come and speak with her before she went, and she, with God's help, would settle up with each of them so that they would hold themselves content. And so she did.

Afterwards, she took leave of her husband and of the holy anchorite, who had told her before the sequence of her going and the great distress that she would suffer along the way and, when all her companions abandoned her, how a broken-backed man would escort her on her way in safety, through the help of our Lord. And so it happened indeed, as it shall be written afterwards.

Then she took her leave of Master Robert and asked him for his blessing, and so took leave of other friends. And then she went on her way to Norwich, and offered at the Trinity, and afterwards she went to Yarmouth, and offered at an image of our Lady, and there she boarded her ship.

And next day they came to a large town called Zierik-zee, where our Lord in his high goodness visited this creature with abundant tears of contrition for her own sins, and sometimes for other people's sins as well. And especially, she had tears of compassion at the memory of our Lord's Passion. And she received communion every Sunday, when time and place were convenient for it, with much weeping and violent sobbing, so that many people marvelled and wondered at the great grace that God worked in his creature.

This creature had eaten no meat and drunk no wine for four years before she left England, and now her confessor directed her, by virtue of obedience, that she should both eat meat and drink wine, and so she did for a little while. Afterwards, she prayed to her confessor to excuse her if she ate no meat, and allow her to do as she wished for what time he pleased.

And soon after, because of prompting by some of her companions, her confessor was displeased because she ate no meat, and so were many of the company. And they were most annoyed because she wept so much and spoke all the time about the love and goodness of our Lord, as much at table as in other places. And so they rebuked her shamefully and chided her harshly, and said they would not put up with her as her husband did when she was at home in England.

And she replied meekly to them, 'Our Lord, Almighty God, is as great a lord here as in England, and I have as great cause to love him here as there – blessed may he be.'

At these words her companions were angrier than they were before, and their anger and unkindness were a matter of great unhappiness to this creature, for they were considered very good men, and she greatly desired their love, if she might have had it to the pleasure of God. And then she said to one of them specially, 'You cause me much shame and hurt.'

He replied, 'I pray God that the devil's death may overtake you soon and quickly,' and he said many more cruel words to her than she could repeat. And soon after, some of the company she trusted best, and also her own maidservant, said she should not accompany them any longer, and they said they would take her maidservant away from her so that she would not be prostituted in her company. And then one of them, who was looking after her money, very angrily left her a noble to go where she liked and shift for herself as well as she could – for with them, they said, she could stay no longer, and they abandoned her that night.

Then, on the next morning, one of her company came to her, a man who got on with her well, who asked her to go to his fellow pilgrims and behave meekly to them, and ask them if she might still travel with them until she came to Constance.

And so she did, and went on with them until she came

41

to Constance with great distress and trouble, for they caused her much shame and reproof as they went along, in various places. They cut her gown so short that it only came a little below her knee, and made her put on some white canvas in a kind of sacking apron, so that she would be taken for a fool, and people would not make much of her or hold her in any repute. They made her sit at the end of the table below all the others, so that she scarcely dared speak a word.

And notwithstanding all their malice, she was held in more esteem than they were, wherever they went. And the good man of the house where they were staying, even though she sat at the end of the table, would always do whatever he could to cheer her up before them all and sent her what he had from his own meal, and that annoyed her companions terribly.

As they travelled towards Constance, they were told they would be harmed and have great trouble unless they had great grace. Then this creature came to a church and went in to pray, and she prayed with all her heart, with much weeping and many tears, for help and succour against their enemies.

Then our Lord said to her mind, 'Don't be afraid, daughter, your party will come to no harm while you are in their company.'

And so – blessed may our Lord be in all his works – they went on in safety to Constance.

Abandoned Abroad

When this creature and her companions had arrived at Constance, she heard tell of an English friar, a master of divinity and the Pope's legate, who was in that city. Then she went to that worthy man and unfolded to him the story of her life from the beginning up to that hour, as near as she could in confession, because he was the Pope's legate and a respected clerk.

And afterwards she told him what trouble she was having with her companions. She also told him what grace God gave her of contrition and compunction, of sweetness and devotion, and of many various revelations which our Lord had revealed to her, and the fear that she had of delusions and deceptions by her spiritual enemies, because of which she lived in great fear, desiring to put them aside and to feel none, if she might withstand them.

And when she had spoken, the worthy clerk gave her words of great comfort, and said it was the work of the Holy Ghost, commanding and charging her to obey them and receive them when God would give them and to have no doubts, for the devil has no power to work such grace in a soul. And also he said he would support her against the ill will of her companions.

Afterwards, when her party pleased, they invited this worthy doctor to dinner. And the doctor told this creature, warning her to sit at table in his presence as she did in his absence, and behave in the same way as she did when he was not there.

When the time had come for them to sit at table, everybody took his place where he liked. The worthy legate and doctor sat first, and then the others, and lastly the said creature, sitting at the end of the table and speaking not a word, as she was wont to do when the legate was not there. Then the legate said to her, 'Why are you not merrier?'

And she sat still and did not answer, as he himself had commanded her to do.

When they had eaten, the company made a great deal of complaint about this creature to the legate, and said absolutely that she could no longer be in their party, unless he would order her to eat meat as they did, and leave off her weeping, and that she should not talk so much of holiness.

Then the worthy doctor said, 'No, sirs, I will not make her eat meat while she can abstain and be the better disposed to love our Lord. Whichever of you all who made a vow to walk to Rome barefoot, I would not dispense him of his vow whilst he might fulfil it, and nor will I order her to eat meat while our Lord gives her strength to abstain. As for her weeping, it is not in my power to restrain it, for it is the gift of the Holy Ghost. As for her talking, I will ask her to stop until she comes somewhere that people will hear her more gladly than you do.'

The company was extremely angry. They gave her over to the legate and said absolutely that they would have nothing more to do with her. He very kindly and benevolently received her as though she had been his mother, and took charge of her money – about twenty pounds – and yet one of them wrongfully withheld about sixteen pounds. And they also withheld her maidservant and would not let her go with her mistress, notwithstanding that she had promised her mistress and assured her that she would not forsake her for any necessity.

And the legate made all arrangements for this creature (and organized for her the exchange of her English money into foreign money), as though she had been his mother. Then this creature went into a church and prayed our Lord to arrange for somebody to escort her. And then our Lord spoke to her and said, 'You shall have a very good help and guide.'

And very soon afterwards there came to her an old man with a white beard. He came from Devonshire, and he said, 'Ma'am, will you ask me, for God's love and for our Lady's, to go with you and be your guide, since your fellow countrymen have forsaken you?'

She asked what his name was.

He said, 'My name is William Wever.'

45

She prayed him, out of reverence of God and of our Lady, to help her in her need, and she would well reward him for his labour. And so they were agreed.

Then she went to the legate and told him how well our Lord had arranged for her, and took her leave of him and of her party who had so unkindly rejected her, and also of her maidservant who was bound to have gone with her. She took leave with a very long face and was very unhappy, because she was in a strange country, and did not know the language or the man who was going to escort her either. And so the man and she went off together in great anxiety and gloom. As they went along together this man said to her, 'I'm afraid you'll be taken from me, and I'll be beaten up because of you and lose my coat.'

She said, 'William, don't be afraid. God will look after us very well.'

And every day this creature remembered the Gospel that tells of the woman who was taken in adultery and brought before our Lord. And then she prayed.

'Lord, as you drove away her enemies, so drive away my enemies, and preserve my chastity that I vowed to you and let me never be defiled, and if I am, Lord, I vow that I will never return to England as long as I live.'

Then they went on day by day and met many excellent people. And they didn't say a bad word to this creature, but gave her and her man food and drink, and the good wives at the lodgings where they put up laid her in their own beds for God's love in many places where they went. And our Lord visited her with great grace of spiritual comfort as she went on her way.

And so God brought her on her way until she came to Bologna. And after she had got there, her former companions who had abandoned her arrived there too. And when they heard tell that she had got to Bologna before them they were amazed, and one of the party came to her asking her to go to his companions and try if they would have her back again in their party. And so she did.

'If you want to travel in our party you must give a new undertaking, which is this: you will not talk of the Gospel where we are, but you will sit and make merry, like us, at all meals.'

She agreed and was received back into their party. Then they went on to Venice and stayed there thirteen weeks. And this creature received communion every Sunday in a great house of nuns – and was very warmly welcomed amongst them – where our merciful Lord Christ Jesus visited this creature with great devotion and plentiful tears, so that the good ladies of the place were greatly amazed at it.

Afterwards it happened, as this creature sat at table with her companions, that she repeated a text of the Gospel which she had learned before with other good words, and then her companions said she had broken her undertaking. And she said, 'Yes, sirs, indeed I can no longer keep this agreement with you, for I must speak of my

Lord Jesus Christ, though all this world had forbidden me.'

And then she took to her chamber and ate alone for six weeks, until the time when our Lord made her so ill that she thought she would die, and then he suddenly made her well again. And all the time her maidservant left her alone and prepared the company's food and washed their clothes, and to her mistress, whom she had promised to serve, she would in no way attend.

Margery's Tears

Also this company, which had excluded the said creature from their table so that she should no longer eat amongst them, arranged a ship for themselves to sail in. They bought containers for their wine and arranged bedding for themselves, but nothing for her. Then she, seeing their unkindness, went to the man they had been to and provided herself with bedding as they had done, and came where they were and showed them what she had done, intending to sail with them in that ship which they had engaged.

Afterwards, as this creature was in contemplation, our Lord warned her in her mind that she should not sail in that ship, and he assigned her another ship, a galley, that she should sail in. Then she told this to some of the company, and they told it to others of their party, and then they dared not sail in the ship which they had arranged. And so they sold off the containers which they had got for their wines, and were very glad to come to the galley where she was, and so, though it was against her will, she went on with them in their company, for they did not dare do otherwise.

When it was time to make their beds they locked up her bedclothes, and a priest who was in her party took a sheet away from this creature, and said it was his. She took God to witness that it was her sheet. Then the priest swore a great oath, by the book in his hand, that she was as false as she might be, and despised her and severely rebuked her.

And so she had great and continual tribulation until she came to Jerusalem. And before she arrived there, she said to them that she supposed they were annoyed with her, 'I pray you, sirs, be in charity with me, for I am in charity with you, and forgive me if I have annoyed you along the way. And if any of you have in any way trespassed against me, God forgive you for it, as I do.'

And so they went on into the Holy Land until they could see Jerusalem. And when this creature saw Jerusalem – she was riding on an ass – she thanked God with all her heart, praying him for his mercy that, just as he had brought her to see this earthly city of Jerusalem, he would grant her grace to see the blissful city of Jerusalem above, the city of heaven. Our Lord Jesus Christ, answering her thought, granted her her desire.

Then for the joy that she had and the sweetness that she felt in the conversation of our Lord, she was on the point of falling off her ass, for she could not bear the sweetness and grace that God wrought in her soul. Then two German pilgrims went up to her and kept her from falling – one of them was a priest, and he put spices in her mouth to comfort her, thinking she was ill. And so they helped her onwards to Jerusalem, and when she arrived there she said, 'Sirs, I beg you, don't be annoyed though I weep bitterly in this holy place where our Lord Jesus Christ lived and died.'

Then they went to the Church of the Holy Sepulchre in Jerusalem, and they were let in on the one day at evensong time, and remained until evensong time on the next day. Then the friars lifted up a cross and led the pilgrims about from one place to another where our Lord had suffered his pains and his Passion, every man and woman carrying a wax candle in one hand. And the friars always, as they went about, told them what our Lord suffered in every place. And this creature wept and sobbed as plenteously as though she had seen our Lord with her bodily eyes suffering his Passion at that time. Before her in her soul she saw him in truth by contemplation, and that caused her to have compassion. And when they came up on to the Mount of Calvary, she fell down because she could not stand or kneel, but writhed and wrestled with her body, spreading her arms out wide, and cried with a loud voice as though her heart would have burst apart, for in the city of her soul she saw truly and freshly how our Lord was crucified. Before her face she heard and saw in her spiritual sight the mourning of our Lady, of St John and Mary Magdalene, and of many others that loved our Lord.

And she had such great compassion and such great

51

pain to see our Lord's pain, that she could not keep herself from crying and roaring though she should have died for it. And this was the first crying that she ever cried in any contemplation. And this kind of crying lasted for many years after this time, despite anything that anyone might do, and she suffered much contempt and much reproof for it. The crying was so loud and so amazing that it astounded people, unless they had heard it before, or else knew the reason for the cryings. And she had them so often that they made her very weak in her bodily strength, and specially if she heard of our Lord's Passion.

And sometimes, when she saw the crucifix, or if she saw a man had a wound, or a beast, whichever it were, or if a man beat a child before her or hit a horse or other beast with a whip, if she saw or heard it, she thought she saw our Lord being beaten or wounded, just as she saw it in the man or in the beast, either in the fields or in the town, and alone by herself as well as among people.

When she first had her cryings at Jerusalem, she had them often, and in Rome also. And when she first came home to England her cryings came but seldom, perhaps once a month, then once a week, afterwards daily, and once she had fourteen in one day, and another day she had seven, just as God would visit her with them, sometimes in church, sometimes in the street, sometimes in her chamber, sometimes in the fields, when God would send them, for she never knew the time nor hour when they would come. And they never came without surpassingly great sweetness of devotion and high contemplation.

And as soon as she perceived that she was going to cry, she would hold it in as much as she could, so that people would not hear it and get annoyed. For some said it was a wicked spirit tormented her; some said it was an illness; some said she had drunk too much wine; some cursed her; some wished she was in the harbour; some wished she was on the sea in a bottomless boat; and so each man as he thought. Other, spiritually inclined men loved her and esteemed her all the more. Some great clerks said our Lady never cried so, nor any saint in heaven, but they knew very little what she felt, nor would they believe that she could not stop herself from crying if she wanted.

And therefore, when she knew that she was going to cry, she held it in as long as she could, and did all that she could to withstand it or else to suppress it, until she turned the colour of lead, and all the time it would be seething more and more in her mind until such time as it burst out. And when the body might no longer endure the spiritual effort, but was overcome with the unspeakable love that worked so fervently in her soul, then she fell down and cried astonishingly loud. And the more that she laboured to keep it in or to suppress it, so much the more would she cry, and the louder.

And thus she did on the Mount of Calvary, as it is written before: she had as true contemplation in the sight of

53

her soul as if Christ had hung before her bodily eye in his manhood. And when through dispensation of the high mercy of our sovereign saviour, Christ Jesus, it was granted to this creature to behold so truly his precious tender body, all rent and torn with scourges, more full of wounds than a dove-cote ever was of holes, hanging upon the cross with the crown of thorns upon his head, his blessed hands, his tender feet nailed to the hard wood, the rivers of blood flowing out plenteously from every limb, the grisly and grievous wound in his precious side shedding out blood and water for her love and her salvation, then she fell down and cried with a loud voice, twisting and turning her body amazingly on every side, spreading her arms out wide as if she would have died, and could not keep herself from crying and these physical movements, because of the fire of love that burned so fervently in her soul with pure pity and compassion.

It is not to be wondered at if this creature cried out and made astonishing expressions, when we may see every day with our own eyes both men and women – some for loss of worldly wealth, some for love of their family or for worldly friendships, through overmuch study and earthly affection, and most of all for inordinate love and physical feeling, if their friends are parted from them – who will cry and roar and wring their hands as if they were out of their wits and minds, and yet they know well enough that they displease God.

And if anybody advises them to leave off their weeping

and crying, they will say that they cannot; they loved their friend so much and he was so gentle and kind to them that they may in no way forget him. How much more might they weep, cry and roar, if their most beloved friends were violently seized in front of their eyes and brought with every kind of reproof before the judge, wrongfully condemned to death, and especially so shameful a death as our merciful Lord suffered for our sake. How would they bear it? No doubt they would both cry and roar and avenge themselves if they could, or else people would say they were no friends.

Alas, alas for sorrow, that the death of a creature who has often sinned and trespassed against his Maker should be so immeasurably mourned and sorrowed over. It is an offence to God and a hindrance to other souls.

And the compassionate death of our Saviour, by which we are all restored to life, is not kept in mind by us unworthy and unkind wretches, nor will we support those whom our Lord has entrusted with his secrets and endued with love, but rather disparage and hinder them as much as we may.

Margery in Jerusalem

When this creature with her companions came to the grave where our Lord was buried, then, as she entered that holy place, she fell down with her candle in her hand, as if she would have died for sorrow. And later she rose up again with great weeping and sobbing, as though she had seen our Lord buried right in front of her. Then she thought she saw our Lady in her soul: how she mourned and how she wept for her son's death, and then was our Lady's sorrow her sorrow.

And so wherever the friars led them in that holy place, she always wept and sobbed astonishingly, and specially when she came to where our Lord was nailed on the cross. There she cried out and wept without control, and could not restrain herself. They also came to a marble stone that our Lord was laid on when he was taken down from the cross, and there she wept with great compassion, remembering our Lord's Passion.

Afterwards she received communion on the Mount of Calvary, and then she wept, she sobbed, she cried out so loudly that it was amazing to hear it. She was so full of holy thoughts and meditations, and holy contemplations in the Passion of our Lord Jesus Christ, and holy conversation in which our Lord conversed with her soul, that she could never express them later, so high and so holy they were. Great was the grace that our Lord showed to this creature for the three weeks that she was in Jerusalem.

Another day, early in the morning, they visited the great hills, and her guides told where our Lord bore the cross on his back, and where his mother met with him, and how she swooned, and how she fell down and he fell down also. And so they went on all the morning until they came to Mount Zion, and all the time this creature wept abundantly for compassion of our Lord's Passion. On Mount Zion is a place where our Lord washed his disciples' feet, and a little way from there he celebrated the Last Supper with his disciples.

And therefore this creature had a great desire to receive communion in that holy place where our merciful Lord Christ Jesus first consecrated his precious body in the form of bread, and gave it to his disciples. And so she was with great devotion, with plenteous tears, and with violent sobbings, for in this place there is plenary remission, and so there is in four other places in the Church of the Holy Sepulchre. One is on the Mount of Calvary; another at the grave where our Lord was buried; the third is at the marble stone that his precious body was laid on when it was taken from the cross; the fourth is where the holy cross was buried; and in many other places of Jerusalem.

And when this creature came to the place where the apostles received the Holy Ghost, our Lord gave her great devotion. Afterwards she went to the place where our Lady was buried, and as she knelt on her knees during the hearing of two masses, our Lord Jesus Christ said to her, 'You do not come here, daughter, for any need except merit and reward, for your sins were forgiven you before you came here, and therefore you come here for the increasing of your reward and merit. And I am well pleased with you, daughter, because you are obedient to Holy Church, and you obey your confessor and follow his counsel, who, by authority of Holy Church, has absolved you of your sins and dispensed you, so that you need not go to Rome or to St James at Compostela, unless you wish to yourself. Notwithstanding all this, I command you in the name of Jesus, daughter, that you go to visit these holy places and do as I bid you, for I am above Holy Church, and I shall go with you and keep you safe.'

Then our Lady spoke to her soul in this way, saying, 'Daughter, you are greatly blessed, for my son Jesus will infuse so much grace into you that the whole world will marvel at you. Don't be ashamed, my beloved daughter, to receive the gifts which my son will give you, for I tell you truly they will be great gifts that he will give you. And therefore, dear daughter, don't be ashamed of him who is your God, your Lord and your love, any more than I was ashamed when I saw him hang on the cross – my sweet son Jesus – to cry and to weep for the pain of my sweet son, Jesus Christ. Nor was Mary Magdalene ashamed to cry and weep for my son's love. And therefore, daughter, if you will be a partaker in our joy, you must be a partaker in our sorrow.'

Such was the sweet conversation that this creature had at our Lady's grave, and a great deal more than she could ever repeat.

Afterwards she rode on an ass to Bethlehem, and when she came to the church and to the crib where our Lord was born, she had great devotion, much conversing in her soul, and high spiritual comfort, with much weeping and sobbing, so that her fellow pilgrims would not let her eat in their company. And so she ate her meals alone by herself.

And then the Grey Friars who had led her from place to place took her in with them and seated her with them at meals, so that she should not eat alone. And one of the friars asked one of her party if that was the Englishwoman who, they had heard tell, spoke with God. And when this came to her knowledge, she knew that it was the truth that our Lord said to her before she left England: 'Daughter, I shall make the whole world wonder at you, and many men and women shall speak of me for love of you, and honour me in you.'

Not for a Hundred Pounds

Another time this creature's companions wanted to go to the River Jordan and would not let her go with them. Then this creature prayed our Lord that she might go with them, and he bade that she should go with them whether they wanted her to or not. And then she set forth by the grace of God and didn't ask their permission. When she came to the River Jordan the weather was so hot that she thought her feet would be burnt because of the heat that she felt.

Afterwards she went on with her fellow pilgrims to Mount Quarentyne, where our Lord fasted for forty days. And there she asked her companions to help her up the mountain, and they said 'no,' because they could scarcely help themselves up. Then she was very miserable because she could not get up the mountain. And just then a Saracen, a good-looking man, happened to come by her, and she put a groat into his hand, making signs to him to take her up the mountain. And quickly the Saracen took her under his arm and led her up the high mountain where our Lord fasted forty days. Then she was dreadfully thirsty and got no sympathy from her fellow pilgrims, but then God, of his high goodness, moved the Grey Friars with compassion, and they comforted her, when her fellow countrymen would not acknowledge her.

And so she was ever more strengthened in the love of our Lord and the more bold to suffer shame and rebukes for his sake in every place she went, because of the grace that God wrought in her of weeping, sobbing and crying out, which grace she could not withstand when God would send it. And always she proved her feelings to be true, and those promises that God had made her while she was in England, and in other places also, came to her in effect just as she had sensed before, and therefore she dared the better receive such speeches and conversation, and act the more boldly in consequence.

Afterwards, when this creature had come down from the Mount, as God willed, she went on to the place where St John the Baptist was born. And later she went to Bethany, where Mary and Martha lived, and to the grave where Lazarus was buried and raised from death to life. And she visited the chapel where our blessed Lord appeared to his blessed mother before all others on the morning of Easter Day. And she stood in the same place where Mary Magdalene stood when Christ said to her, 'Mary, why are you weeping?' And so she was in many more places than are written here, for she was three weeks in Jerusalem and in places thereabouts. And she always had great devotion as long as she was in that country.

And the friars of the Church of the Holy Sepulchre

were very welcoming to her and gave her many great relics, wanting her to remain among them if she had wished, because of the belief they had in her. The Saracens also made much of her, and conveyed and escorted her about the country wherever she wanted to go. And she found all people good and gentle to her, except her own countrymen.

And as she went from Jerusalem to Ramleh, she would have liked to return again to Jerusalem, because of the great grace and spiritual comfort that she felt when she was there, and to gain herself more pardon. And then our Lord commanded her to go to Rome, and so on home to England, and said to her, 'Daughter, as often as you say or think "Worshipped be all those holy places in Jerusalem that Christ suffered bitter pain and passion in," you shall have the same pardon as if you were there with your bodily presence, both for yourself and for all those that you will give it to.'

And as she travelled to Venice, many of her companions were very ill, and all the time our Lord said to her, 'Don't be afraid, daughter, no one will die in the ship that you are in.'

And she found her feelings completely true. And when our Lord had brought them all to Venice again in safety, her fellow countrymen abandoned her and went off, leaving her alone. And some of them said that they would not go with her for a hundred pounds.

When they had gone away from her, then our Lord

Jesus Christ – who always helps in need and never forsakes his servant who truly trusts in his mercy – said to his creature, 'Don't be afraid, daughter, because I shall provide for you very well, and bring you in safety to Rome and home again to England without any disgrace to your body, if you will be clad in white clothes, and wear them as I said to you while you were in England.'

Then this creature, being in great unhappiness and doubt, answered in her mind, 'If you are the spirit of God that speaks in my soul, and I may prove you to be a true spirit through counsel of the church, I shall obey your will; and if you bring me to Rome in safety, I shall wear white clothes, even though all the world should wonder at me, for your love.'

'Go forth, daughter, in the name of Jesus, for I am the spirit of God, which shall help you in your every need, go with you, and support you in every place – and therefore, do not mistrust me. You never found me deceiving, nor did I ever bid you do anything except what is worship of God and profit to your soul if you will obey; and I shall infuse into you great abundance of grace.'

Just then, as she looked to one side, she saw a poor man sitting there, who had a great hump on his back. His clothes were all very much patched, and he seemed a man of about fifty. Then she went up to him and said, 'Good man, what's wrong with your back?'

He said, 'It was broken in an illness, ma'am.'

She asked what his name was, and where he was from.

He said his name was Richard, and he was from Ireland. Then she thought of her confessor's words, who was a holy anchorite, as is written before, who spoke to her while she was in England in this way: 'Daughter, when your own companions have abandoned you, God will provide a broken-backed man to escort you wherever you want to go.'

Then she with a glad spirit said to him, 'Good Richard, guide me to Rome, and you shall be rewarded for your labour.'

'No, ma'am,' he said, 'I know very well that your countrymen have abandoned you, and therefore it would be difficult for me to escort you. Your fellow countrymen have both bows and arrows with which they can defend both you and themselves, and I have no weapon except a cloak full of patches. And yet I fear that my enemies will rob me, and perhaps take you away from me and rape you; and therefore I dare not escort you, for I would not, for a hundred pounds, have you suffer any disgrace while you were with me.'

And then she replied, 'Richard, don't be afraid. God will look after both of us very well, and I shall give you two nobles for your trouble.'

Then he agreed and set off with her.

Margery Goes to Rome

On one occasion, as this creature was in church at Assisi, there was exhibited our Lady's kerchief – which she wore here on earth – with many lights and great reverence. Then this creature had great devotion. She wept, she sobbed, she cried, with great abundance of tears and many holy thoughts. She was there also on Lammas Day, when there is great pardon with plenary remission, in order to obtain grace, mercy and forgiveness for herself, for all her friends, for all her enemies, and for all the souls in purgatory.

And there was a lady who had come from Rome to obtain her pardon. Her name was Margaret Florentyne, and she had with her many Knights of Rhodes, many gentlewomen, and a very fine equipage.

Then Richard, the broken-backed man, went to her, asking her if this creature could go with her to Rome – and himself too – so as to be kept safe from the danger of thieves. And then that worthy lady received them into her party and let them go with her to Rome, as God willed. When this creature came to Rome, those who were her fellow pilgrims before and excluded her from their company were also in Rome, and when they heard tell that such a woman had arrived they were greatly surprised at how she came there safely.

And then she went and got her white clothes and was clad all in white, just as she was commanded to do years before in her soul by revelation, and now it was fulfilled in effect.

Then this creature was taken in at the Hospital of St Thomas of Canterbury in Rome, and there she received communion every Sunday with great weeping, violent sobbing and loud crying, and was highly beloved by the Master of the Hospital and all his brethren.

And then, through the stirring of her spiritual enemy, there came a priest, who was held to be a holy man in the Hospital and also in other places in Rome, and who was one of her companions and one of her own countrymen. And notwithstanding his holiness, he spoke so badly of this creature and slandered her name so much in the Hospital that, through his evil tongue, she was put out of the Hospital, so that she could no longer be shriven or receive communion there.

For Fairer, for Fouler

As this creature was in the church of the Holy Apostles at Rome on St Lateran's Day, the Father of Heaven said to her, 'Daughter, I am well pleased with you, inasmuch as you believe in all the sacraments of Holy Church and in all faith involved in that, and especially because you believe in the manhood of my son, and because of the great compassion that you have for his bitter Passion.'

The Father also said to this creature, 'Daughter, I will have you wedded to my Godhead, because I shall show you my secrets and my counsels, for you shall live with me without end.'

Then this creature kept silence in her soul and did not answer to this, because she was very much afraid of the Godhead; and she had no knowledge of the conversation of the Godhead, for all her love and affection were fixed on the manhood of Christ, and of that she did have knowledge and would not be parted from that for anything.

She had so much feeling for the manhood of Christ, that when she saw women in Rome carrying children in their arms, if she could discover that any were boys, she would cry, roar and weep as if she had seen Christ in his childhood. And if she could have had her way, she would often have taken the children out of their mothers' arms and kissed them instead of Christ. And if she saw a handsome man, she had great pain to look at him, lest she might see him who was both God and man. And therefore she cried many times and often when she met a handsome man, and wept and sobbed bitterly for the manhood of Christ as she went about the streets of Rome, so that those who saw her were greatly astonished at her, because they did not know the reason.

Therefore it was not surprising if she was still and did not answer the Father of Heaven, when he told her that she should be wedded to his Godhead. Then the Second Person, Christ Jesus, whose manhood she loved so much, said to her, 'What do you say to my Father, Margery, daughter, about these words that he speaks to you? Are you well pleased that it should be so?'

And then she would not answer the Second Person, but wept amazingly much, desiring to have himself still, and in no way to be parted from him. Then the Second Person in the Trinity answered his Father for her, and said, 'Father, excuse her, for she is still only young and has not completely learned how she should answer.'

And then the Father took her by the hand [spiritually] in her soul, before the Son and the Holy Ghost, and the Mother of Jesus, and all the twelve apostles, and St Katherine and St Margaret and many other saints and holy virgins, with a great multitude of angels, saying to her soul, 'I take you, Margery, for my wedded wife, for fairer, for fouler, for richer, for poorer, provided that you are humble and meek in doing what I command you to do. For, daughter, there was never a child so kind to its mother as I shall be to you, both in joy and sorrow, to help you and comfort you. And that I pledge to you.'

And then the Mother of God and all the saints that were present there in her soul prayed that they might have much joy together. Then this creature with high devotion, with great abundance of tears, thanked God for this spiritual comfort, holding herself in her own feeling very unworthy of any such grace as she felt, for she felt many great comforts, both spiritual comforts and bodily comforts. Sometimes she sensed sweet smells in her nose; they were sweeter, she thought, than any earthly sweet thing ever was that she smelled before, nor could she ever tell how sweet they were, for she thought she might have lived on them if they had lasted.

Sometimes she heard with her bodily ears such sounds and melodies that she could not hear what anyone said to her at that time unless he spoke louder. These sounds and melodies she had heard nearly every day for twenty-five years when this book was written, and especially when she was in devout prayer, also many times while she was at Rome, and in England too.

She saw with her bodily eyes many white things flying all about her on all sides, as thickly in a way as specks in a sunbeam; they were very delicate and comforting, and

69

the brighter the sun shone, the better she could see them. She saw them at many different times and in many different places, both in church and in her chamber, at her meals and at her prayers, in the fields and in town, both walking and sitting. And many times she was afraid what they might be, for she saw them at night in darkness as well as in daylight. Then when she was afraid of them, our Lord said to her, 'By this token, daughter, believe it is God who speaks in you, for wherever God is, heaven is, and where God is, there are many angels, and God is in you and you are in him. And therefore, don't be afraid, daughter, for these betoken that you have many angels around you, to keep you both day and night so that no devil shall have power over you, nor evil men harm you.'

Then from that time forward she used to say when she saw them coming: *'Benedictus qui venit in nomine Domini.'**

Our Lord also gave her another token which lasted about sixteen years, and increased ever more and more, and that was a flame of the fire of love – marvellously hot and delectable and very comforting, never diminishing but ever increasing; for though the weather were never so cold she felt the heat burning in her breast and at her heart, as veritably as a man would feel the material fire if he put his hand or his finger into it.

When she first felt the fire of love burning in her breast she was afraid of it, and then our Lord answered in her

---

* 'Blessed is he who comes in the name of the Lord'

mind and said, 'Daughter, don't be afraid, because this heat is the heat of the Holy Ghost, which will burn away all your sins, for the fire of love quenches all sins. And you shall understand by this token that the Holy Ghost is in you, and you know very well that wherever the Holy Ghost is, there is the Father, and where the Father is, there is the Son, and so you have fully in your soul all of the Holy Trinity. Therefore you have great cause to love me well, and yet you shall have greater cause than you ever had to love me, for you shall hear what you never heard, and you shall see what you never saw, and you shall feel what you never felt.

'For, daughter, you are as sure of the love of God, as God is God. Your soul is more sure of the love of God than of your own body, for your soul will part from your body, but God shall never part from your soul, for they are united together without end. Therefore, daughter, you have as great reason to be merry as any lady in this world; and if you knew, daughter, how much you please me when you willingly allow me to speak in you, you would never do otherwise, for this is a holy life and the time is very well spent. For, daughter, this life pleases me more than wearing the coat of mail for penance, or the hair-shirt, or fasting on bread and water; for if you said a thousand *paternosters* every day you would not please me as much as you do when you are in silence and allow me to speak in your soul.'

On Homely Terms

'Fasting, daughter, is good for young beginners, and discreet penance, especially what their confessor gives them or enjoins them to do. And to pray many beads is good for those who can do no better, yet it is not perfect. But it is a good way towards perfection. For I tell you, daughter, those who are great fasters and great doers of penance want it to be considered the best life; those also who give themselves over to saying many devotions would have that to be the best life; and those who give very generous alms would like that considered the best life.

'And I have often told you, daughter, that thinking, weeping, and high contemplation is the best life on earth. You shall have more merit in heaven for one year of thinking in your mind than for a hundred years of praying with your mouth; and yet you will not believe me, for you will pray many beads whether I wish it or not. And yet, daughter, I will not be displeased with you whether you think, say or speak, for I am always pleased with you.

'And if I were on earth as bodily as I was before I died on the cross, I would not be ashamed of you, as many other people are, for I would take you by the hand amongst the people and greet you warmly, so that they would certainly know that I loved you dearly.

'For it is appropriate for the wife to be on homely terms with her husband. Be he ever so great a lord and she ever so poor a woman when he weds her, yet they must lie together and rest together in joy and peace. Just so must it be between you and me, for I take no heed of what you have been but what you would be, and I have often told you that I have clean forgiven you all your sins.

'Therefore I must be intimate with you, and lie in your bed with you. Daughter, you greatly desire to see me, and you may boldly, when you are in bed, take me to you as your wedded husband, as your dear darling, and as your sweet son, for I want to be loved as a son should be loved by the mother, and I want you to love me, daughter, as a good wife ought to love her husband. Therefore you can boldly take me in the arms of your soul and kiss my mouth, my head, and my feet as sweetly as you want. And as often as you think of me or would do any good deed to me, you shall have the same reward in heaven as if you did it to my own precious body which is in heaven, for I ask no more of you but your heart, to love me who loves you, for my love is always ready for you.'

Then she gave thanks and praise to our Lord Jesus Christ for the high grace and mercy that he showed to her, unworthy wretch.

This creature had various tokens in her hearing. One was a kind of sound as if it were a pair of bellows blowing

73

in her ear. She – being dismayed at this – was warned in her soul to have no fear, for it was the sound of the Holy Ghost. And then our Lord turned that sound into the voice of a dove, and afterwards he turned it into the voice of a little bird which is called a redbreast, that often sang very merrily in her right ear. And then she would always have great grace after she heard such a token. She had been used to such tokens for about twenty-five years at the time of writing this book.

Then our Lord Jesus Christ said to his creature, 'By these tokens you may well know that I love you, for you are to me a true mother and to all the world, because of that great charity which is in you; and yet I am cause of that charity myself, and you shall have great reward for it in heaven.'

Margery in Poverty

Afterwards, while this creature was in Rome, our Lord bade her give away all her money and make herself destitute for his love. And she immediately, with a fervent desire to please God, gave away such money as she had, and such also as she had borrowed from the broken-backed man who went with her. When he found out how she had given away his money, he was greatly moved and displeased that she had given it away, and spoke very sharply to her. And then she said to him, 'Richard, by the grace of God, we shall come home to England very well. And you shall come to me in Bristol in Whitsun week, and there I shall pay you well and truly, by the grace of God, for I trust faithfully that he who bade me give it away for his love will help me to pay it back.'

And so he did.

After this creature had thus given away her money and had not a penny to help herself with, as she lay in St Marcellus's Church in Rome, thinking and concentrating as to where she could get her living, inasmuch as she had no silver to keep herself with, our Lord answered to her mind and said, 'Daughter, you are not yet as poor as I was when I hung naked on the cross for your love, for you have clothes on your body and I had none. And you have advised other people to be poor for my sake, and therefore you must follow your own advice.

'But do not be afraid, daughter, for money will come to you, and I have promised you before that I would never fail you. I shall pray my own mother to beg for you, for you have many times begged for me, and for my mother also. And therefore do not be afraid. I have friends in every country, and I shall cause my friends to comfort you.'

When our Lord had talked sweetly to her soul in this way, she thanked him for this great comfort, completely trusting that it would be as he said. Afterwards she got up and went out into the street and by chance met a good man. And so they fell into edifying conversation as they went along together, and she repeated to him many good tales and many pious exhortations until God visited him with tears of devotion and compunction, so that he was highly comforted and consoled. And then he gave her money, by which she was relieved and comforted for a good while.

Then one night she saw in a vision how our Lady, she thought, sat at table with many worthy people and asked for food for her. And then this creature thought that our Lord's words were fulfilled spiritually in that vision, for he promised this creature a little before that he would pray his mother to beg for her.

And very shortly after this vision she met up with a worthy lady, Dame Margaret Florentyne, the same lady who brought her from Assisi to Rome, and neither of them could understand the other very well, except by signs and tokens and a few common words. And then the lady said to her, '*Margerya in poverté?*'

She, understanding what the lady meant, answered, '*Yea, grand poverté, madame.*'

Then the lady commanded her to eat with her every Sunday and seated her at her own table above herself, and served her her food with her own hands. Then this creature sat and wept bitterly, thanking our Lord that she was thus encouraged and cherished for his love by those who could not understand her language.

When they had eaten, the good lady used to give her a hamper with other stuff which she could make stew from for herself, enough to serve her with two days' food, and filled her bottle with good wine. And sometimes she gave her eight bolendine coins as well.

Then another man in Rome, who was called Marcelle, asked her to meals two days a week. His wife was about to have a baby, and she very much wanted this creature to be godmother to her child when it was born, but she did not stay in Rome long enough.

And also there was a pious single lady who gave this creature her food on Wednesdays. Other days, when she was not provided for, she begged for her food from door to door.

Margery travels home from Rome, and soon sets off on another trip, this time to Santiago, before returning to England and travelling around the country, despite the great personal danger.

Margery Arrested

Afterwards she went on to Leicester with a good man, Thomas Marchale, of whom is written before. And there she came into a fine church where she beheld a crucifix, which was piteously portrayed and lamentable to behold, and through beholding of which, the Passion of our Lord entered her mind, whereupon she began to melt and utterly dissolve with tears of pity and compassion. Then the fire of love kindled so quickly in her heart that she could not keep it secret for, whether she liked it or not, it caused her to break out in a loud voice and cry astonishingly, and weep and sob very terribly, so that many men and women wondered at her because of it.

When it was overcome, and she was going out of the church door, a man took her by the sleeve and said, 'Woman, why are you weeping so bitterly?'

'Sir,' she said, 'it is not to be told to you.'

And so she and the good man, Thomas Marchale, went on and found lodgings for themselves and ate a meal there. When they had eaten, she asked Thomas Marchale to write a letter and send it to her husband, so that he might fetch her home. And while the letter was being

written, the innkeeper came up to her room in great haste
and took away her bag, and ordered her to come quickly
and speak with the Mayor. And so she did. Then the
Mayor asked her from which part of the country she
came, and whose daughter she was.

'Sir,' she said, 'I am from Lynn in Norfolk, the daughter
of a good man of the same Lynn, who has been five times
mayor of that worshipful borough, and also an alderman
for many years; and I have a good man, also a burgess
of the said town of Lynn, for my husband.'

'Ah,' said the Mayor, 'St Katherine told of what kindred
she came, and yet you are not alike, for you are a false
strumpet, a false Lollard, and a false deceiver of the
people, and therefore I shall have you in prison.'

And she replied, 'I am as ready, sir, to go to prison for
God's love, as you are ready to go to church.'

When the Mayor had rebuked her for a long time and
said many evil and horrible words to her, and she – by
the grace of Jesus – had reasonably answered him in
everything that he could say, then he commanded the
gaoler's man to lead her to prison. The gaoler's man,
having compassion for her with weeping tears, said to
the Mayor, 'Sir, I have no place to put her in, unless I
put her in among men.'

Then she – moved with compassion for the man who
had compassion for her, praying for grace and mercy to
that man as to her own soul – said to the Mayor, 'I beg
you, sir, not to put me among men, so that I may keep

my chastity, and my bond of wedlock to my husband, as I am bound to do.'

And then the gaoler himself said to the Mayor, 'Sir, I will undertake to keep this woman in my own safekeeping until you want to see her again.'

Then there was a man from Boston, who said to the good wife where she was lodging, 'Truly,' he said, 'in Boston this woman is held to be a holy woman and a blessed woman.'

Then the gaoler took her into his custody, and led her home to his own house and put her into a fine room, locking the door with a key, and ordering his wife to keep the key safe. Nevertheless, he let her go to church when she wished, and let her eat at his own table, and made her very welcome for our Lord's love – thanks be to Almighty God for it.

'English, if you please'

Then the Steward of Leicester, a good-looking man, sent for the said creature to the gaoler's wife, and she – because her husband was not at home – would not let her go to any man, Steward or otherwise. When the gaoler knew about this he came himself, and brought her before the Steward. As soon as he saw her, the Steward spoke Latin to her, many priests standing about to hear what she would say, and other people too. She said to the Steward, 'Speak English, if you please, for I do not understand what you are saying.'

The Steward said to her, 'You lie most falsely, in plain English.'

Then she replied to him, 'Sir, ask what question you will in English, and through the grace of my Lord Jesus Christ I shall answer you very reasonably.'

And then he asked many questions, to which she answered readily and reasonably, so that he could get no cause against her.

Then the Steward took her by the hand and led her into his chamber, and spoke many foul, lewd words to her, intending and desiring, as it seemed to her, to overcome her and rape her. And then she had great fear and great sorrow, begging him for mercy. She said, 'Sir, for the reverence of Almighty God, spare me, for I am a man's wife.'

And then the Steward said: 'You shall tell me whether you get this talk from God or from the devil, or else you shall go to prison.'

'Sir,' she said, 'I am not afraid to go to prison for my Lord's love, who suffered much more for my love than I may for his. I pray you, do as you think best.'

The Steward, seeing her boldness in that she was not afraid of any imprisonment, struggled with her, making filthy signs and giving her indecent looks, through which he frightened her so much that she told him how she had her speech and conversing from the Holy Ghost and not from her own knowledge.

And then he, completely astonished at her words, left off his lewdness, saying to her as many a man had done before, 'Either you are a truly good woman or else a truly wicked woman,' and delivered her up again to her gaoler, and he led her home again with him.

Afterwards they took two of her companions who went with her on pilgrimage – one was Thomas Marchale, aforesaid, the other a man from Wisbech – and put them both in prison because of her. Then she was grieved and sorry for their distress, and prayed to God for their deliverance. And then our merciful Lord Christ Jesus said to his creature, 'Daughter, I shall, for your love, so dispose for them that the people will be very glad to let them go, and not detain them for long.'

And on the next day following, our Lord sent such storms of thunder and lightning, and continuous rain, that all the people in the town were so afraid they didn't know what to do. They feared it was because they had put the pilgrims in prison.

And then those who governed the town went in great haste and took out the two pilgrims, who had lain in prison all the night before, leading them to the Guildhall, there to be examined before the Mayor and the reputable men of the town, compelling them to swear if the said creature were a woman of true faith and true belief, chaste and pure of body, or not.

As far as they knew, they swore, as certainly as God should help them at the Day of Judgement, that she was a good woman of true faith and true belief, pure and chaste in all her conduct as far as they knew, in manner and expression, in word and deed.

And then the Mayor let them go wherever they wished. And soon the storm ceased, and the weather was fair – worshipped be our Lord. Those pilgrims were glad that they were released, and dared not stay in Leicester any longer, but went ten miles away and stayed there, so that they could get information as to what would be done with the said creature. For when they were both put in prison, they had told her themselves that they supposed that, if the Mayor could have his way, he would have her burnt.

Margery on Trial

On a Wednesday, the said creature was brought into a church of All Saints in Leicester, in which place, before the high altar, were seated the Abbot of Leicester with some of his canons, and the Dean of Leicester, a worthy cleric. There were also many friars and priests; also the Mayor of the same town with many other lay people. There were so many people that they stood upon stools to look at her and marvel at her.

The said creature knelt down, saying her prayers to Almighty God that she might have grace, wit and wisdom, so to answer that day as might be most pleasure and honour to him, most profit to her soul, and best example to the people.

Then a priest came to her and took her by the hand, and brought her before the Abbot and his assessors sitting at the altar, who made her swear on a book that she should answer truly to the Articles of the Faith, just as she felt about them. And first they repeated the blessed sacrament of the altar, charging her to say exactly what she believed about it.

Then she said, 'Sirs, I believe in the sacrament of the

altar in this way: that whatever man has taken the order of priesthood, be he never so wicked a man in his manner of life, if he duly say those words over the bread that our Lord Jesus Christ said when he celebrated the Last Supper sitting among his disciples, I believe that it is his very flesh and his blood, and no material bread; nor may it ever be unsaid, be it once said.'

And so she went on answering on all the articles, as many as they wished to ask her, so that they were well pleased.

The Mayor, who was her deadly enemy, said, 'Truly, she does not mean with her heart what she says with her mouth.'

And the clerics said to him, 'Sir, she answers us very well.'

Then the Mayor severely rebuked her and repeated many reproving and indecent words, which it is more fitting to conceal than express.

'Sir,' she said, 'I take witness of my Lord Jesus Christ, whose body is here present in the sacrament of the altar, that I never had part of any man's body in this world in actual deed by way of sin, except my husband's body, to whom I am bound by the law of matrimony, and by whom I have borne fourteen children. For I would have you know, sir, that there is no man in this world that I love so much as God, for I love him above all things, and, sir, I tell you truly, I love all men in God and for God.'

Also, furthermore, she said plainly to his face, 'Sir, you are not worthy to be a mayor, and that shall I prove by

Holy Writ, for our Lord God said himself before he would take vengeance on the cities, "I shall come down and see," and yet he knew all things. And that was for nothing else, sir, but to show men such as you are that you should not carry out punishments unless you have prior knowledge that they are appropriate. And, sir, you have done quite the contrary to me today, for, sir, you have caused me much shame for something I am not guilty of. I pray God forgive you it.'

Then the Mayor said to her, 'I want to know why you go about in white clothes, for I believe you have come here to lure away our wives from us, and lead them off with you.'

'Sir,' she said, 'you shall not know from my mouth why I go about in white clothes; you are not worthy to know it. But, sir, I will gladly tell it to these worthy clerks by way of confession. Let them consider whether they will tell it to you.'

Then the clerks asked the Mayor to go down from among them with the other people. And when they had gone, she knelt on her knees before the Abbot, and the Dean of Leicester, and a Preaching Friar, a worthy cleric, and told these three clerics how our Lord by revelation warned her and bade her wear white clothes before she went to Jerusalem.

'And so I have told my confessors. And therefore they have charged me that I should go about like this, for they dare not go against my feelings for fear of God; and if they dared, they would do so very gladly. And therefore, sirs, if the Mayor wants to know why I go about in white, you may say, if you please, that my confessors order me to do so; and then you will tell no lies, yet he will not know the truth.'

So the clerics called the Mayor up again, and told him in confidence that her confessors had charged her to wear white clothes, and she had bound herself in obedience to them.

Then the Mayor called her to him, saying, 'I will not let you go from here in spite of anything you can say, unless you go to my Lord Bishop of Lincoln for a letter, inasmuch as you are in his jurisdiction, so that I may be discharged of responsibility for you.'

She said, 'Sir, I certainly dare speak to my Lord of Lincoln, for I have been very kindly received by him before now.'

And then other men asked her if she were in charity with the Mayor, and she said, 'Yes, and with all whom God has created.' And then she, bowing to the Mayor and weeping tears, prayed him to be in charity with her, and forgive her anything in which she had displeased him. And he spoke fine words to her for a while, so that she believed all was well, and that he was her good friend, but afterwards she well knew it was not so.

And thus she had leave from the Mayor to go to my Lord Bishop of Lincoln, and fetch a letter by which the Mayor should be excused responsibility.

The Bishop's Letter

So she went first to Leicester Abbey and into the church, and as soon as the Abbot had espied her he, out of his goodness, with many of his brethren, came to welcome her.

When she saw them coming, at once in her soul she beheld our Lord coming with his apostles, and she was so ravished into contemplation with sweetness and devotion, that she could not stand until they came, as courtesy demanded, but leaned against a pillar in the church and held on to it tightly for fear of falling, for she would have stood and she could not, because of the abundance of devotion which was the reason that she cried and wept very bitterly.

When she had overcome her crying, the Abbot asked his brethren to take her in with them and comfort her, and so they gave her very good wine and were extremely nice to her.

Then she got herself a letter from the Abbot to my Lord of Lincoln, putting on record what controversy she had been in during the time that she was in Leicester. And the Dean of Leicester was also ready to provide a record and act as witness for her, for he had great confidence that our Lord loved her, and therefore he comforted her very highly in his own place.

And so she took leave of her said son [Thomas Marchale], intending to travel to Lincoln with a man called Patrick, who had been with her to Santiago previously. And at this time he was sent by the said Thomas Marchale, from Melton Mowbray to Leicester, to inquire and see how things stood with the same creature. For the said Thomas Marchale was very afraid that she would have been burnt, and therefore he sent this man Patrick to find out the truth.

And so she and Patrick, together with many good folk of Leicester who had come to encourage her, thanking God who had preserved her and given her victory over her enemies, went out to the edge of the town, and there they gave her a good send-off, promising her that, if she ever came back, she would receive a much better welcome amongst them than she had before.

Then she had forgotten and left behind in the town a staff made with a piece of Moses' rod, which she had brought back from Jerusalem, and would not have lost for forty shillings. Then Patrick went into the town again for her staff and her bag and happened to meet the Mayor, and the Mayor would have put him in prison, so that in the end he got away with difficulty and left her bag there.

The said creature was waiting for this man in a blind

woman's house in a very gloomy mood, dreading what had happened to him because he was so long. At last this man came riding past where she was. When she saw him she cried, 'Patrick, son, where have you been so long away from me?'

'Yes, yes, mother,' he said, 'I have been in great danger for you. I was on the point of being put in prison because of you, and the Mayor has greatly harassed me because of you, and he has taken away your bag from me.'

'Ah, good Patrick,' she said, 'don't be upset, for I shall pray for you, and God will well reward you for your trouble; it is all for the best.'

Then Patrick set her upon his horse and brought her home to his own house in Melton Mowbray where Thomas Marchale was, as previously mentioned, who took her down from the horse, highly thanking God that she was not burnt. So they rejoiced in our Lord all that night.

And afterwards she went on to the Bishop of Lincoln, where he was staying at that time. She, not exactly knowing where he was, met a very respectable man with a furred hood, a very worthy officer of the Bishop's, who said to her, 'Woman, don't you recognize me?'

'No, sir,' she said, 'truly.'

'And yet you have been beholden to me,' he said, 'because I was once very good to you.'

'Sir, I trust that what you did you did for God's love, and therefore I hope he will well reward you. And I beg you to excuse me, for I take little heed of a man's good looks or of his face, and therefore I forget him much the sooner.'

And then he kindly told her where she would find the Bishop, and so she got herself a letter from the Bishop to the Mayor of Leicester, admonishing him that he should not trouble her, nor hinder her from coming and going when she wanted.

Then there occurred great storms of thunder and lightning and heavy rain, so that people believed it was for revenge of the said creature, greatly desiring that she had been out of that part of the country. And she would in no way leave until she had her bag again.

When the said Mayor received the Bishop's letter, he sent her her bag and let her go in safety wherever she wanted.

Delicious Against her Will

Through listening to holy books and through listening to holy sermons, she was always increasing in contemplation and holy meditation. It would be impossible to write all the holy thoughts, holy speeches, and high revelations which our Lord showed to her, both concerning herself and other men and women, and also concerning many souls, some to be saved and some to be damned.

This was a great punishment and a sharp chastisement to her. To know of those who would be saved, she was very glad and joyful, because she longed as much as she dared for all men to be saved; and when our Lord revealed to her any who would be damned, she had great pain. She would not hear it, nor believe that it was God who showed her such things, and put it out of her mind as much as she could. Our Lord blamed her for this, and bade her believe that it was his high mercy and his goodness to reveal to her his secret counsels, saying to her mind, 'Daughter, you must hear of the damned as well as of the saved.'

She would give no credence to the counsel of God, but rather believed it was some evil spirit out to deceive her.

Then for her forwardness and her unbelief, our Lord withdrew from her all good thoughts and all good recollections of holy speeches and conversation, and the high contemplation which she had been used to before, and allowed her to have as many evil thoughts as she previously had good thoughts. And this affliction lasted twelve days altogether, and just as previously she had four hours in the morning of holy speeches and confabulation with our Lord, so she now had as many hours of foul thoughts and foul recollections of lechery and all uncleanness, as though she would have prostituted herself with all manner of people.

And so the devil deluded her, dallying with her with accursed thoughts, just as our Lord dallied with her previously with holy thoughts. And just as before she had many glorious visions and high contemplation upon the manhood of our Lord, upon our Lady, and upon many other holy saints, even so now she had horrible and abominable visions – despite anything she could do – of seeing men's genitals, and other such abominations.

She saw, as she really thought, various men of religion, priests and many others, both heathen and Christian, coming before her eyes so that she could not avoid them or put them out of her sight, and showing her their naked genitals.

And with that the devil ordered her in her mind to choose which of them she would have first, and she must prostitute herself to them all.

And he said she liked one of them better than all the others. She thought he spoke the truth; she could not say no; and she had to do his bidding, and yet she would not have done it for all this world. But yet she thought it should be done, and she thought that these horrible sights and accursed thoughts were delicious to her against her will. Wherever she went or whatever she did, these accursed thoughts remained with her. When she would see the sacrament, say her prayers, or do any other good deed, such abomination was always put into her mind. She was shriven and did all that she could, but she found no release, until she was nearly in despair. It cannot be written what pain she felt, and what sorrow she was in.

Then she said, 'Alas, Lord, you have said before that you would never forsake me. Where is now the truthfulness of your word?'

And immediately afterwards her good angel came to her, saying, 'Daughter, God has not forsaken you, nor ever shall forsake you, as he has promised you. But because you do not believe that it is the spirit of God that speaks in your soul and reveals to you his secret counsels, of some that shall be saved and some that shall be damned, therefore God chastises you in this way, and this chastising shall endure twelve days until you will believe that it is God who speaks to you and no devil.'

Then she said to her angel, 'Ah, I pray you, pray for me to my Lord Jesus Christ, that he will vouchsafe to take from me these accursed thoughts, and speak to me as he did before now, and I shall make a promise to God that I shall believe that it is God who has spoken to me before, for I may no longer endure this great pain.'

Her angel said to her again, 'Daughter, my Lord Jesus will not take it away from you until you have suffered it twelve days, for he wishes that you should know by that means whether it is better that God speak to you or the devil. And my Lord Christ Jesus is never the angrier with you, though he allow you to feel this pain.'

So she suffered that pain until twelve days were passed, and then she had as holy thoughts, as holy reflections, and as holy desires, as holy speeches and conversation with our Lord Jesus Christ as she ever had before, our Lord saying to her, 'Daughter, now believe indeed that I am no devil.'

Then she was filled with joy, for she heard our Lord speaking to her as he used to do. Therefore she said, 'I shall believe that every good thought is the speech of God. Blessed may you be, Lord, that you do not disdain to comfort me again. I would not, Lord, for all this world suffer such another pain as I suffered these twelve days, for I thought I was in hell – blessed may you be that it is past. Therefore, Lord, I will now lie still and be obedient to your will. I pray you, Lord, speak in me what is most pleasing to you.'

Margery's Husband

It happened one time that the husband of the said creature – a man of great age, over sixty years old – would have come down from his chamber bare-foot and bare-legged, and he slithered, or else missed his footing, and fell to the ground from the stairs, with his head twisted underneath him, seriously broken and bruised, so much so that he had five linen plugs in the wounds in his head for many days while his head was healing.

And, as God willed, it was known to some of his neighbours how he had fallen down the stairs, perhaps through the din and the rushing of his falling. And so they came in to him and found him lying with his head twisted under himself, half alive, all streaked with blood, and never likely to have spoken with priest nor clerk, except through high grace and miracle.

Then the said creature, his wife, was sent for, and so she came to him. Then he was taken up and his head was sewn, and he was ill for a long time after, so that people thought he would die. And then people said, if he died, his wife deserved to be hanged for his death, for as much as she could have looked after him and did not. They did not live together, nor did they sleep together, for – as it is written before – they both with one assent and with the free will of each other had made a vow to live chaste. And therefore, to avoid all risks, they lived in different places, where no suspicion could be had of their lack of chastity. For, at first, they lived together after they had made their vow, and then people slandered them, and said they enjoyed their lust and their pleasure as they did before the making of their vow. And when they went out on pilgrimage, or to see and speak with other spiritually-minded creatures, many evil folk whose tongues were their own hurt, lacking the fear and love of our Lord Jesus Christ, believed and said that they went rather to woods, groves or valleys, to enjoy the lust of their bodies, where people should not espy it or know it.

Knowing how prone people were to believe evil of them, and desiring to avoid all occasion as far as they properly could, by mutual good will and consent, they parted from each other as regards their board and lodging, and went to board in different places. And this was the reason that she was not with him, and also so that she should not be hindered from her contemplation. And therefore, when he had fallen and was seriously hurt, as is said before, people said, if he died, it was proper that she should answer for his death. Then she prayed to our Lord that her husband might live a year, and she be delivered from slander, if it were his pleasure.

Our Lord said to her mind, 'Daughter, you shall have

your boon, for he shall live, and I have performed a great miracle for you that he was not dead. And I bid you take him home, and look after him for my love.'

She said, 'No, good Lord, for I shall then not attend to you as I do now.'

'Yes, daughter,' said our Lord, 'you shall have as much reward for looking after him and helping him in his need at home, as if you were in church to say your prayers. And you have said many times that you would gladly look after me. I pray you now, look after him for love of me, for he has sometime fulfilled both your will and my will, and he has made your body freely available to me, so that you should serve me and live chaste and clean, and therefore I wish you to be available to help him in his need, in my name.'

'Ah, Lord,' said she, 'for your mercy, grant me grace to obey your will, and fulfil your will, and never let my spiritual enemies have any power to hinder me from fulfilling your will.'

Then she took her husband home with her and looked after him for years afterwards, as long as he lived. She had very much trouble with him, for in his last days he turned childish and lacked reason, so that he could not go to a stool to relieve himself, or else he would not, but like a child discharged his excrement into his linen clothes as he sat there by the fire or at the table – wherever it was, he would spare no place. And therefore her labour was all the greater, in washing and wringing, and so were her expenses for keeping a fire going. All this hindered her a very great deal from her contemplation, so that many times she would have disliked her work, except that she thought to herself how she in her young days had had very many delectable thoughts, physical lust, and inordinate love for his body. And therefore she was glad to be punished by means of the same body, and took it much the more easily, and served him and helped him, she thought, as she would have done Christ himself.

A Vision of the Crucifixion

Another time she saw in her contemplation our Lord Jesus Christ bound to a pillar, and his hands were bound above his head. And then she saw sixteen men with sixteen scourges, and each scourge had eight tips of lead on the end, and each tip was full of sharp prickles, as if it had been the rowel of a spur. And those men with the scourges made a covenant that each of them should give our Lord forty strokes.

When she saw this piteous sight, she wept and cried very loudly, as if she would have burst for sorrow and pain. And when our Lord was severely beaten and scourged, the Jews loosed him from the pillar, and gave him his cross to bear on his shoulder. And then she thought that our Lady and she went by another way to meet with him, and when they met with him, they saw him carrying the heavy cross with great pain, it was so heavy and so huge that he could scarcely bear it.

And then our Lady said to him, 'Ah, my sweet son, let me help to carry that heavy cross.'

And she was so weak that she could not, but fell down and swooned, and lay as still as if she had been a dead

woman. Then the creature saw our Lord fall down by his
mother, and comfort her as he could with many sweet
words. When she heard the words and saw the compassion that the mother had for the son, and the son for the
mother, then she wept, sobbed and cried as though
she would have died, for the pity and compassion that
she had for that piteous sight, and the holy thoughts
that she had in the meantime, which were so subtle and
heavenly that she could never describe them afterwards,
as she had them in feeling.

Later she went forth in contemplation, through the
mercy of our Lord Jesus Christ, to the place where he
was nailed to the cross. And then she saw the Jews with
great violence tear off of our Lord's precious body a cloth
of silk, which had stuck and hardened so firmly and
tightly to our Lord's body with his precious blood, that
it pulled away with it all the skin from his blessed body
and renewed his precious wounds, and made the blood
to run down all around on every side. Then that precious
body appeared to her sight as raw as something that was
newly flayed out of its skin, most pitiful to behold. And
so she had a new sorrow, so that she wept and cried very
bitterly.

And soon after, she beheld how the cruel Jews laid his
precious body on the cross, and then took a long nail, all
rough and coarse, and set it on one hand, and with great
violence and cruelty they drove it through his hand. His
blessed mother beholding – and this creature – how his

precious body shrank and drew together with all the sinews and veins in that precious body for the pain that it suffered and felt, they sorrowed and mourned and sighed very grievously.

Then she saw, with her spiritual eye, how the Jews fastened ropes on to the other hand – for the sinews and veins were so shrunken with pain that it would not reach to the hole that they had drilled for it – and they pulled on it to make it reach the hole. And so her pain and her sorrow ever increased. And later they pulled his blessed feet in the same way.

And then she thought, in her soul, she heard our Lady say to the Jews, 'Alas, you cruel Jews, why do you treat my sweet son like this, and he never did you any harm? You fill my heart full of sorrow.'

And then she thought the Jews spoke back roughly to our Lady, and moved her away from her son.

Then the said creature thought that she cried out at the Jews, and said, 'You accursed Jews, why are you killing my Lord Jesus Christ? Kill me instead, and let him go.'

And then she wept and cried surpassingly bitterly, so that many people in the church were astonished. She straightaway saw them take up the cross with our Lord's body hanging on it, and make a great noise and cry; and they lifted it up from the earth a certain distance, and then let the cross fall down into the mortise. And then our Lord's body shook and shuddered, and all the joints of that blissful body burst and broke apart, and his precious wounds ran down with rivers of blood on every side, and so she had ever more reason for more weeping and sorrowing.

And then she heard our Lord, hanging on the cross, say these words to his mother, 'Woman, see your son, St John the Evangelist.'

Then she thought our Lady fell down and swooned, and St John took her up in his arms and comforted her with sweet words, as well as he could. This creature then said to our Lord, as it seemed to her, 'Alas, Lord, you are leaving here a mother full of care. What shall we do now, and how shall we bear this great sorrow that we shall have for your love?'

And then she heard the two thieves speaking to our Lord, and our Lord said to the one thief, 'This day you shall be with me in paradise.'

Then she was glad of that answer, and prayed our Lord, for his mercy, that he would be as gracious to her soul when she should pass out of this world as he was to the thief – for she was worse, she thought, than any thief.

And then she thought our Lord commended his spirit into his father's hands, and with that he died. Then she thought she saw our Lady swoon and fall down and lie still, as if she had been dead. Then this creature thought that she ran all round the place like a mad woman, crying and roaring. And later she came to our Lady, and fell down on her knees before her, saying to her, 'I pray you, Lady, cease from your sorrowing, for your son is dead and out of pain, and I think you have sorrowed enough. And Lady, I will sorrow for you, for your sorrow is my sorrow.'

Then she thought she saw Joseph of Arimathea take down our Lord's body from the cross, and lay it before our Lady on a marble stone. Our Lady had a kind of joy when her dear son was taken down from the cross and laid on the stone before her. And then our blessed Lady bowed down to her son's body and kissed his mouth, and wept so plentifully over his blessed face, that she washed away the blood from his face with the tears of her eyes.

And then this creature thought she heard Mary Magdalene say to our Lady, 'I pray you, Lady, give me leave to handle and kiss his feet, for at these I get grace.'

At once our Lady gave leave to her and all those who were there, to offer what worship and reverence they wished to that precious body. And Mary Magdalene soon took our Lord's feet, and our Lady's sisters took his hands, the one sister one hand and the other sister the other hand, and wept very bitterly in kissing those hands and those precious feet. And the said creature thought that she continually ran to and fro, as if she were a woman without reason, greatly desiring to have had the precious body by herself alone, so that she might have wept enough in the presence of that precious body, for she thought she would have died with weeping and mourning for his death, for love that she had for him.

And at once she saw St John the Evangelist, Joseph of

Arimathea, and other friends of our Lord, come and want to bury our Lord's body, and they asked our Lady that she would allow them to bury that precious body. Our sorrowful Lady said to them, 'Sirs, would you take away from me my son's body? I might never look upon him enough while he lived. I pray you, let me have him now he is dead, and do not part my son and me from each other. And if you will bury him in any case, I pray you, bury me with him, for I may not live without him.'

And then this creature thought that they asked our Lady so beautifully, until at last our Lady let them bury her dear son with great worship and great reverence, as was fitting for them to do.

A Good Hot Drink of Gruel and Spiced Wine

When our Lord was buried, our Lady fell down in a swoon as she would have come from the grave, and St John took her up in his arms, and Mary Magdalene went on the other side, to support and comfort our Lady as much as they could. Then the said creature, desiring to remain still by the grave of our Lord, mourned, wept, and sorrowed with loud crying for the tenderness and compassion that she had of our Lord's death, and the many mournful desires that God put into her mind at that time. Because of this, people wondered at her, marvelling at what was the matter with her, for they little knew the cause. She thought she would never have departed from there, but desired to have died there and been buried with our Lord. Later the creature thought she saw our Lady going homewards again, and, as she went, many good women came to her and said, 'Lady, we are very sorry that your son is dead, and that our people have done him so much shame.'

And then our Lady, bowing down her head, thanked them very meekly by her looks and expression, for she could not speak, her heart was so full of grief.

Then this creature thought, when our Lady had come home and was laid down on a bed, that she made for our Lady a good hot drink of gruel and spiced wine, and brought it to her to comfort her, and then our Lady said to her, 'Take it away, daughter. Give me no food but my own child.'

The creature replied, 'Ah, blessed Lady, you must comfort yourself, and cease from your sorrowing.'

'Ah, daughter, where should I go, or where should I live without sorrow? I tell you, there was certainly never any woman on earth who had such great cause to sorrow as I have, for there was never woman in this world who bore a better child, nor a meeker to his mother, than my son was to me.'

And she thought she soon heard our Lady cry with a lamentable voice and say, 'John, where is my son, Jesus Christ?'

And St John answered and said, 'Dear Lady, you well know that he is dead.'

'Ah, John,' she said, 'that is a very sorrowful counsel for me.'

The creature heard this answer as clearly, in the understanding of her soul, as she would understand one man speaking to another. And soon the creature heard St Peter knocking at the door and St John asked who was there. Peter answered, 'I, sinful Peter, who have forsaken my Lord Jesus Christ.' St John would have made him come in, and Peter would not, until our Lady told him to come in. And then Peter said, 'Lady, I am not worthy to come in to you,' and was still outside the door.

Then St John went to our Lady and told her that Peter was so abashed that he dared not come in. Our Lady told St John to go back quickly to St Peter and bid him come in to her. And then this creature, in her spiritual sight, beheld St Peter come before our Lady and fall down on his knees, with great weeping and sobbing, and say, 'Lady, I beg your forgiveness, for I have forsaken your beloved son and my sweet master, who loved me so well, and therefore, Lady, I am never worthy to look upon him, or you either, except by your great mercy.'

'Ah, Peter,' said our Lady, 'don't be afraid, for, though you have forsaken my sweet son, he never forsook you, Peter, and he shall come again and comfort us all indeed; for he promised me, Peter, that he would come again on the third day and comfort me. Ah, Peter,' said our Lady, 'I shall think it a very long time, until that day comes that I may see his blessed face.'

Then our Lady lay still on her bed, and heard how the friends of Jesus made their lament for the sorrow that they had. And always our Lady lay still, mourning and weeping with sorrowful expression, and at last, Mary Magdalene and our Lady's sisters took their leave of our Lady, in order to go and buy ointment, so that they might anoint our Lord's body with it.

Then this creature was left alone with our Lady and thought it a thousand years until the third day came; and that day she was with our Lady in a chapel where our Lord Jesus Christ appeared to her and said, '*Salve, sancta parens.*' ('Hail, holy parent.')

And then this creature thought in her soul that our Lady said, 'Are you my sweet son, Jesus?'

And he said, 'Yes, my blessed mother, I am your son, Jesus.'

Then he took up his blessed mother and kissed her very sweetly.

And then this creature thought that she saw our Lady feeling and searching all over our Lord's body, and his hands and his feet, to see if there were any soreness or any pain. And she heard our Lord say to his mother, 'Dear mother, my pain is all gone, and now I shall live for ever more. And mother, so shall your pain and your sorrow be turned into very great joy. Mother, ask what you will, and I shall tell you.'

And when he had allowed his mother to ask what she wished and had answered her questions, then he said, 'Mother, by your leave, I must go and speak with Mary Magdalene.'

Our Lady said, 'That is well done, for, son, she has very great sorrow over your absence. And, I pray you, do not be long from me.'

These spiritual sights and understandings caused the creature to weep, to sob and to cry very loudly, so that she could not control or restrain herself on Easter Day and other days when our Lord would visit her with his grace – blessed and worshipped may he be.

And soon after, this creature was – in her contemplation – with Mary Magdalene, mourning and seeking our Lord at the grave, and heard and saw how our Lord Jesus Christ appeared to her in the likeness of a gardener, saying, 'Woman, why are you weeping?'

Mary, not knowing who he was, all enflamed with the fire of love, replied to him, 'Sir, if you have taken away my Lord, tell me, and I shall take him back again.'

Then our merciful Lord, having pity and compassion on her, said, 'Mary.'

And with that word she – knowing our Lord – fell down at his feet, and would have kissed his feet, saying, 'Master.'

Our Lord said to her, 'Touch me not.'

Then this creature thought that Mary Magdalene said to our Lord, 'Ah, Lord, I see you don't want me to be as homely with you as I have been before,' and looked very miserable.

'Yes, Mary,' said our Lord, 'I will never forsake you, but I shall always be with you, without end.'

And then our Lord said to Mary Magdalene, 'Go, tell my brethren and Peter that I have risen.'

And then this creature thought that Mary went with great joy, and it was a great marvel to her that Mary rejoiced for, if our Lord had spoken to her as he did to

Mary, she thought she could never have been happy. That was when she would have kissed his feet, and he said, 'Touch me not.' This creature had such great grief and sorrow at those words that, whenever she heard them in any sermon, as she did many times, she wept, sorrowed and cried as though she would have died, for the love and desire that she had to be with our Lord.

Revelations Are Hard
Sometimes to Understand

While the said creature was occupied with the writing of this treatise, she had many holy tears and much weeping, and often there came a flame of fire about her breast, very hot and delectable; and also, he that was writing for her could sometimes not keep himself from weeping.

And often in the meantime, when this creature was in church, our Lord Jesus Christ with his glorious mother, and many saints as well, came into her soul and thanked her, saying that they were well pleased with the writing of this book. And she also heard many times a voice of a sweet bird singing in her ear, and often she heard sweet sounds and melodies that surpassed her wit to tell of them. And she was many times ill while this treatise was being written, and, as soon as she would set about the writing of this treatise, then in a sudden way she was hale and healthy. And often she was commanded to make herself ready in all haste.

On one occasion, as she lay at her prayers in the church during the time of Advent before Christmas, she thought in her heart that she wished that God, of his goodness, would make Master Aleyn to preach a sermon as well as he could. And as soon as she had thought in this way, she heard our Sovereign Lord Christ Jesus saying in her soul, 'Daughter, I know very well what you are thinking now about Master Aleyn, and I tell you truly that he shall preach a very holy sermon. And see that you believe steadfastly the words that he shall preach, as though I preached them myself, for they shall be words of great solace and comfort to you, for I shall speak in him.'

When she had heard this answer, she went and told it to her confessor and two other priests whom she greatly trusted. And when she had told them her feeling, she was sorry, for fear as to whether he would speak as well as she had felt or not – for revelations are hard sometimes to understand.

And sometimes those that people think were revelations are deceits and illusions, and therefore it is not appropriate to give credence too readily to every stirring, but wait steadfastly and prove if they be sent from God. Nevertheless, as for this feeling of this creature, it was very truth, shown in experience, and her fear and her heaviness of heart turned into great spiritual comfort and gladness.

Sometimes she was greatly depressed about her feelings – when she did not know how they should be understood for many days together, because of the dread that she had of deceptions and delusions – so that she thought she wished her head had been struck from her body until God, of his goodness, explained them to her mind.

For sometimes, what she understood physically was to be understood spiritually, and the fear that she had of her feelings was the greatest scourge that she had on earth; and especially when she had her first feelings; and that fear made her most meek, for she had no joy in the feeling until she knew by experience whether it was true or not.

But ever blessed may God be, for he made her always more mighty and more strong in his love and in his fear, and gave her increase of virtue, with perseverance.

Here ends this treatise, for God took him to his mercy who wrote the first copy of this book. And though he did not write clearly or openly to our manner of speaking, he in his own way of writing and spelling made true sense, which – through the help of God, and of herself who experienced all this treatise in feeling and acting – is now truly drawn out of that copy into this little book.